He has made everything beautiful in its time.
He has also set eternity in the hearts of men;
yet they cannot fathom what God has
done from beginning to end.

ECCLESIASTES 3:11 (EMPHASIS ADDED)

Bless you, Derek and Kirestina!

Don Richardson

ETERNITY
IN THEIR
HEARTS

DON
RICHARDSON

Regal

From Gospel Light
Ventura, California, U.S.A.

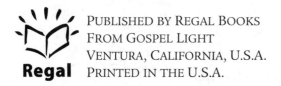
PUBLISHED BY REGAL BOOKS
FROM GOSPEL LIGHT
VENTURA, CALIFORNIA, U.S.A.
PRINTED IN THE U.S.A.

Regal Books is a ministry of Gospel Light, a Christian publisher dedicated to serving the local church. We believe God's vision for Gospel Light is to provide church leaders with biblical, user-friendly materials that will help them evangelize, disciple and minister to children, youth and families.

It is our prayer that this Regal book will help you discover biblical truth for your own life and help you meet the needs of others. May God richly bless you.

For a free catalog of resources from Regal Books/Gospel Light, please call your Christian supplier or contact us at 1-800-4-GOSPEL *or* www.regalbooks.com.

Second Edition, 1984
Third Edition, 2005

Library of Congress Cataloging-in-Publication Data
The Library of Congress has cataloged the second edition as follows:
Richardson, Don 1935-
    Eternity in their hearts.

    Jesus Christ—Miscellanea. 2. Religion. I. Title.
BT304.9.R53 1984 266   84-2036
ISBN 0-8307-3837-1

            4   5   6   7   8   9   10   /   10   09   08   07

Rights for publishing this book in other languages are contracted by Gospel Light Worldwide, the international nonprofit ministry of Gospel Light. Gospel Light Worldwide also provides publishing and technical assistance to international publishers dedicated to producing Sunday School and Vacation Bible School curricula and books in the languages of the world. For additional information, visit www.gospellightworldwide.org; write to Gospel Light Worldwide, P.O. Box 3875, Ventura, CA 93006; or send an e-mail to info@gospellightworldwide.org.

Contents

PART I

A World Prepared for the Gospel

—The Melchizedek Factor—

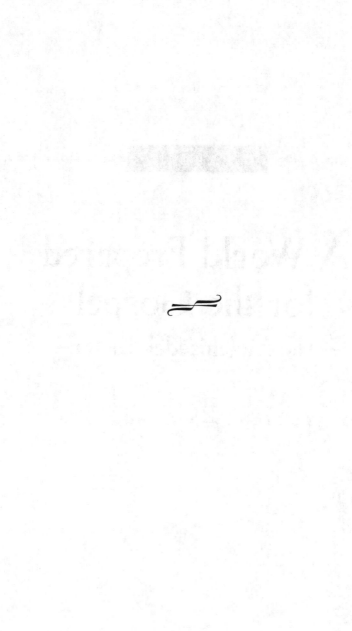

Peoples of the Vague God

THE ATHENIANS

*Sometime during the sixth century before Christ, in a council
chamber on Mars Hill, Athens . . .*

"Tell us, Nicias, what advice has the Pythian oracle sent with you? Why
has this plague come upon us? And why did our numerous sacrifices
avail nothing?"

Cool-eyed Nicias faced the council president squarely. "The priestess
declares that our city lies under a terrible curse. A certain god has placed
this curse upon us because of King Megacles's grievous crime of treachery against the followers of Cylon."

"Yes, yes! I recall now," said another council member grimly.
"Megacles obtained the surrender of Cylon's followers with a promise of
amnesty. Then he promptly violated his own word and slew them! But god

still holds this crime against us? We have atoning sacrifices to all the gods!"

"Not so," replied Nicias. "The priestess says her god still remains unappeased."

"Who could he be?" the elders asked, eyeing Nicias incredulously.

"That I cannot tell you," Nicias said. "The oracle herself seems not to know his name. She said only that . . ."

Nicias paused, surveying the anxious faces of his colleagues. Meanwhile, the tumult of a thousand dirges echoed from the stricken city around them.

Nicias continued: "We must send a ship at once to Knossos, on the island of Crete, and fetch a man named Epimenides here to Athens. The priestess assures me that he will know how to appease that offended god, thus delivering our city."

"Is there no man of sufficient wisdom here in Athens?" blurted an indignant elder. "Must we appeal for help to a . . . a foreigner?"

"If you know a man of sufficient wisdom in Athens, summon him," said Nicias. "If not, let us simply do as the oracle commands."

Cold wind—cold as if chilled by the terror in Athens—swept through the white marble council chamber on Mars Hill. One elder after another pulled his magisterial robe around his shoulders and weighed Nicias's words.

"Go on our behalf, my friend," said the president of the council. "Fetch this Epimenides, if he will hear your plea. And if he delivers our city we will reward him."

Other members of the council concurred. The calm-voiced Nicias arose, bowed before the assembly, and left the chamber. Descending Mars Hill, he headed for the harbor at Piraeus, two leagues distant by the Bay of Phaleron. A ship stood at anchor.

Epimenides stepped briskly ashore at Piraeus, followed by Nicias. The two men set out at once for Athens, gradually recovering their "land legs" after the long sea journey from Crete. As they entered the already world-famous "city of philosophers," signs of the plague were everywhere. But Epimenides noticed something else—

"Never have I seen so many gods!" the Cretan exclaimed to his guide, blinking in amazement. Phalanxes of idols lined both sides of the road from Piraeus. Still other gods in the hundreds festooned a rocky escarpment called the acropolis. A later generation of Athenians would build the Parthenon there.

"How many gods does Athens have?" Epimenides added.

"Several hundred at least!" Nicias replied.

"Several hundred!" Epimenides exclaimed. "Gods must be easier to find here than men!"[1]

"Well said!" Councilman Nicias chuckled. "Who knows how many proverbs men have coined about 'Athens, the city glutted with gods.' As well haul rock to a quarry as bring another god to our city!"

Nicias stopped in his tracks, pondering his own words. "And yet," he began thoughtfully, "the Pythian oracle declares that we Athenians have yet another god to reconcile. And you, Epimenides, are to provide the necessary liaison. Apparently, in spite of what I have said, we Athenians still do need another god!"

Suddenly Nicias threw back his head and laughed. "For the life of me, Epimenides, I cannot guess who this other god could be. We Athenians are the world's foremost collectors of gods! We have already ransacked the theologies of many peoples around us, gathering every deity we can possibly transport to our city by cart or by ship!"

"Perhaps that is your problem," said Epimenides mysteriously.

Nicias blinked at Epimenides without comprehension. How he itched for clarification of that final remark. But something in Epimenides's demeanor hushed him. Moments later they came to an ancient marble-floored stoa near the council chamber on Mars Hill. Word of their arrival had already reached the elders of Athens. The council sat waiting.

"Epimenides, we are grateful for your—" began the president of the assembly.

"Learned elders of Athens, there is no need to thank me." Epimenides interrupted. "Tomorrow at sunrise bring a flock of sheep, a band of stonemasons, and a large supply of stones and mortar to the grassy slope at the foot of this sacred rock. The sheep must all be healthy, and of different colors—some white, some black. And you must prevent them from grazing after their night's rest. They must be *hungry* sheep! I will now rest from my journey. Call me at dawn."

Members of the council exchanged curious glances as Epimenides strode across the stoa to a quiet alcove, pulled his cloak around him for a blanket, and sat down to meditate.

The president turned to a junior member of the council. "See that all is done as he commands," he ordered.

"The sheep are here," said the junior member meekly. Epimenides, tousled and drowsy with sleep, emerged from his resting place and followed the messenger to a grassy slope at the base of Mars Hill. Two flocks—one of black and white sheep and one of councilmen, shepherds and stonemasons—stood waiting beneath a rising sun. Hundreds of citizens, haggard from another night of nursing the plague-stricken and mourning the dead, climbed surrounding hillocks and watched in suspense.

"Learned elders," Epimenides began, "you have already expended great effort in offering sacrifice to your numerous gods, yet all has proved futile. I am now about to offer sacrifices based upon three assumptions rather different from yours. My first assumption . . ."

Every eye fixed upon the tall Cretan; every ear tuned itself to catch his next word.

". . . is that there is still another god concerned in the matter of this plague—a god whose name is unknown to us, and who is therefore not represented by any idol in your city. Secondly, I am going to assume also that this god is great enough—and good enough—to do something about the plague, if only we invoke his help."

"Invoke a god whose name is unknown?" blurted an elder. "Is that possible?"

"The third assumption is my answer to your question," Epimenides countered. "That assumption is a very simple one. Any god great enough and good enough to do something about the plague is probably also great enough and good enough to smile upon us in our ignorance—if we *acknowledge* our ignorance and call upon him!"

Murmurs of approval mingled with the bleating of hungry sheep. Never had the elders of Athens heard this line of reasoning before. But why, they wondered, must the sheep be of different colors?

"Now!" called Epimenides, "prepare to release the sheep upon this sacred slope! Once you have released them, permit each animal to graze where it will. But let a man follow each animal and watch it closely." Then, looking up to heaven, Epimenides prayed in a very rich and supremely confident voice: "O thou unknown god! Behold the plague afflicting this city! And if indeed you feel compassion to forgive and help us, behold this flock of sheep! Reveal your willingness to respond, I plead, by causing any sheep that pleases you to lie down upon the grass instead of grazing. Choose white if white pleases; black if black delights. And those you choose we sacrifice to you—acknowledging our pitiful ignorance of your name!"

Epimenides sat down upon the grass, bowed his head and waved a signal to shepherds guarding the flock. Slowly the shepherds stepped aside. Quickly, eagerly, the sheep spread out across the hillside and began to graze. Epimenides, meanwhile, sat still as a statue, eyes to the ground.

"It's hopeless," a frowning councilman muttered under his breath. "It's early morning, and I've seldom seen a flock so eager to graze. Not a one will choose to rest until its belly's full, and who will then believe 'twas a god that caused it to recline?"

"Epimenides must have chosen this time of day on purpose, then!" responded Nicias. "Only thus may we know that a sheep which lies down does so by the will of this unknown god and not by its own inclination!"

Nicias had hardly finished speaking when a shepherd shouted, "Look!" Every eye turned to see a choice ram buckle its knees and settle onto the grass.

"And here's another!" roared a startled councilman, beside himself with wonder. Within minutes a number of choice sheep lay resting on grass too succulent for any hungry herbivore to resist—under normal circumstances!

"If only one rested, we'd have said it must be sick!" the council president exclaimed. "But this! This can only be an *answer*!"

Turning with awe-filled eyes, he said to Epimenides, "What shall we do now?"

"Separate the sheep that are resting," the Cretan replied, raising his head for the first time since he had called upon his unknown god, "and mark the place where each one lay. Then let your stonemasons build altars—one altar on each animal's resting place!"

Enthusiastic masons set to work mortaring stones. By late afternoon the mortar was sufficiently hardened. Every altar stood ready for use.

"Which god's name shall we engrave upon these altars?" asked an over-eager junior councilman. All heads turned to hear the Cretan's reply.

"Name?" replied Epimenides thoughtfully. "The Deity whose help we seek has been pleased to respond to our admission of *ignorance*. If now we pretend to be knowledgeable by engraving a name when we have not the slightest idea what His name may be, I fear we shall only offend Him!"

"We must not take that chance," the president or the council agreed. "But surely there must be some appropriate way to—to *dedicate* each altar before it is used."

"You are right, learned elder," Epimenides said with a rare smile. "There is a way. Simply inscribe the words *agnosto theo*—to an unknown god—upon the side of each altar. Nothing more is necessary."

The Athenians engraved the words as their Cretan counselor advised. Then they sacrificed each "dedicated" sheep upon the altar marking the spot where that sheep rested. Night fell. By dawn the next day the plague's deadly grip upon the city had already loosened. Within a week, the stricken recovered. Athens overflowed with praise to Epimenides's "unknown God" and to Epimenides himself, for bringing such amazing help in such an inventive manner. Thankful citizens placed garlands of flowers around that huddle of unpretentious altars on the side of Mars Hill. Later they carved a statue of Epimenides in a sitting position and placed it before one of their temples.[2]

With the passage of time, however, the people of Athens began to forget the mercy which Epimenides's "unknown God" had bestowed upon them. At length they neglected His altars on the slope below Mars

Hill. They returned to the worship of the several hundred gods who had proved helpless to remove the curse from their city. Vandals demolished some of the altars and pried stones loose from others. Grass and moss encroached upon the ruins until . . .

One day two elders who remembered the significance of the altars paused among them on the way home from council. Leaning upon their staffs, they gazed wistfully upon the creeper-covered relics. One elder removed a patch of moss and read the ancient inscription hidden beneath: "'Agnosto theo.' Demas—remember?"

"How could I forget?" Demas replied. "I was the junior member of council who stayed up all night to make sure the flock, the stones, the mortar and the masons would all be ready by sunrise!"

"And I," responded the other elder, "was that over-eager junior member who suggested that each altar should have the name of some god engraved upon it! How foolish of me!"

The speaker paused, deep in thought. Then he added, "Demas, you will think me sacrilegious, but I cannot suppress my feeling that if only Epimenides's 'unknown God' would reveal Himself openly to us we might soon dispense with all these others!" The bearded elder waved his staff with mild contempt toward rank beyond rank of deaf-mute idols— more now than ever—lining the crest of acropolis.

"If ever He should reveal Himself," said Demas thoughtfully, "how will our people know that He is no stranger but a God who has already participated in the affairs of our city?"

"I think there is only one way," the first elder replied. "We must seek to preserve at least one of these altars as evidence for posterity. And the story of Epimenides must somehow be kept alive among our traditions."

"A great idea!" Demas glowed. "Look! This one is still in fair condition. We'll hire masons to polish it up. And tomorrow we'll remind the entire council of that long-ago victory over the plague. We'll get a motion passed to include the maintenance of at least this altar among the perennial expenditures of our city!"

The two elders shook hands in agreement. Then, locked arm in arm, they hobbled off down the path, jubilantly clicking their staffs against the stones of Mars Hill.

The foregoing is based mainly upon a tradition recorded as history by Diogenes Laertius, a Greek author of the third century A.D., in a classical work called *The Lives of Eminent Philosophers*.[3] The basic elements in Diogenes's account are: Epimenides, a Cretan hero, responded to a request borne to him from Athens by a man called Nicias, asking him to advise the city of Athens in the matter of a plague. Arriving in Athens, Epimenides obtained a flock of black and white sheep and released them on Mars Hill, instructing men to follow the sheep and mark the places where any of them lay down.

Epimenides's apparent purpose was to give any god concerned in the matter of the plague an opportunity to reveal his willingness to help by causing sheep that pleased him to lie down to rest as a sign that he would accept those sheep if they were offered in sacrifice. Since there would have been nothing unusual about sheep lying down apart from one of their usual grazing periods, presumably Epimenides conducted his experiment early in the morning, when sheep would be at their hungriest.

A number of sheep rested, and the Athenians offered them in sacrifice upon unnamed altars built especially for the purpose. Thus the plague lifted from the city.

Readers of the Old Testament will recall that a hero named Gideon, seeking knowledge of God's will, "put out the fleece." Epimenides did Gideon one better—he put out the whole flock!

According to a passage in Plato's *Laws*, Epimenides at the same time also prophesied that 10 years in the future a Persian army would come against Athens. He assured the Athenians, however, that their Persian foes "will return back again with all their hopes frustrated, and after suffering more woes than they inflict." This prophecy was fulfilled. The council, for its part, offered Epimenides a talent of coins for his services, but he refused to accept payment. "The only reward I desire," he said, "is that we here and now establish a treaty of friendship between Athens and Knossos." The Athenians agreed. Ratifying a treaty with Knossos, they then gave Epimenides safe transport back to his island home.

(Plato, in that same passage, pays tribute to Epimenides as "that inspired man," and credits him as one of the great men who helped mankind rediscover inventions lost during "The Great Flood.")

Other details in this account concerning the cause of the curse are from an editor's footnote on Aristotle's *The Art of Rhetoric*, book 3, 17:10, found in the Loeb Classical Library, translated by J. H. Freese and published in Cambridge, Massachusetts. The explanation that none other than the Pythian oracle instructed the Athenians to summon Epimenides is found in the previously mentioned reference from Plato's *Laws*.

Diogenes Laertius himself does not mention that the words *agnosto theo* were inscribed upon Epimenides's altars. He states only that "altars may be found in different parts of Attica with no name inscribed upon them, which are memorials of this atonement."

Two other ancient writers, however—Pausanias in his *Description of Greece* and Philostratus in his *Appolonius of Tyana*—refer to "altars to an unknown god" implying that an inscription to that effect was engraved upon them.

That such an inscription was engraved upon at least one altar in Athens is verified by a first-century historian named Luke. Describing the adventures of Paul, the famous Christian apostle, Luke mentions an encounter awesomely illuminated by the foregoing story of Epimenides: "While Paul was waiting . . . in Athens," Luke began, "he was greatly distressed to see that the city was full of idols" (Acts 17:16).

If Athens boasted several hundred gods in Epimenides's time, by Paul's day there may have been hundreds more. Idolatry, by its very nature, has a built-in "inflation factor." Once men reject the one omniscient, omnipotent and omnipresent God in favor of lesser deities, they eventually discover—to their frustration—*that it takes an infinite number of lesser deities to fill the true God's shoes!*

When Paul saw Athens prostituting man's sacred privilege of worship upon mere wood and stone, horror gripped him! He took immediate action. First: "He reasoned in the synagogue with the Jews and the God-fearing Greeks" (Acts 17:17).

Not that Jews and God-fearing Greeks were the ones practicing idolatry! Not at all. They were, however, the people most responsible to oppose the idolatry rampant in their city.

Perhaps Paul found them so accustomed to scenes of idolatry that they could no longer mount a persuasive offensive against it. In any case, Paul launched his own offensive. He reasoned also, Luke says, "in the marketplace day by day with those who happened to be there" (Acts 17:17).

Who *did* happen to be there? And how did they react? Luke explains: "A group of Epicurean and Stoic philosophers began to dispute with him. Some of them asked, 'What is this babbler trying to say?'"

Even an apostle can experience difficulties in cross-cultural communication!

"Others remarked, 'He seems to be advocating foreign gods'" (Acts 17:18).

Why this latter comment? Doubtless the philosophers heard Paul speak of *Theos*—God. *Theos* was a familiar term to them. They, however, commonly used it not as a personal name, but as a general term for any deity—just as "man" in English means any man and is not considered suitable as a personal name for any one man.

The philosophers must have known, however, that Xenophanes, Plato and Aristotle—three great philosophers—used *Theos* as a personal name for one Supreme God in their writings.[4]

Two centuries after Plato's and Aristotle's time, translators of the Septuagint—the first Greek version of the Old Testament—grappled with a major problem: Could a suitable equivalent for the Hebrew name for God, Elohim, be found in the Greek language? They rejected the name *Zeus*. Even though Zeus was called "king of the gods," pagan theologians had chosen to make Zeus the offspring of two other gods, Cronus and Rhea. An offspring of other beings cannot equal Elohim, who is uncreated. Finally the translators recognized the above three philosophers' fortuitous use of *Theos* as a personal Greek name for the Almighty. *Theos*, in this special usage, was a name still unencrusted with barnacles of error! They adopted it. So also Paul adopted *Theos* for his New Testament preaching and writing!

It may therefore have been not *Theos*, but the unfamiliar name *Jesus* which caused the philosophers to think that Paul was "advocating foreign gods." Perhaps also they were astonished that anyone would want to bring still another god to Athens, god capital of the world! Athenians, after all, must have needed something equivalent to the Yellow Pages just to keep tabs on the many deities already represented in their city!

How did Paul respond to the suggestion that he was advocating superfluous foreign gods in a city already glutted with gods?

Jesus Christ had already given Paul a masterful formula for coping with cross-cultural communication problems like this one at Athens. Speaking through a vision so persuasive that it filled Paul with new insights and so bright it left him temporarily blind, Jesus had said: "I am sending you to open their eyes and turn them from darkness to light" (Acts 26:17-18).

Jesus' logic was faultless. If people are to turn from darkness to light, their eyes must first be opened to see the difference between darkness and light. And what does it take to open someone's eyes?

An eye-opener!

But where could Paul—born a Jew, reborn a Christian—find an eye-opener for the truth about the supreme God in idol-infested Athens? He could hardly expect a religious system totally committed to polytheism to contain an acknowledgment that monotheism is better.

Ah, but as Paul "walked around and observed" (Acts 17:23) he found something in the midst of "the system" that was not "of the system"—an altar not associated with any idol! An altar bearing the curious inscription "to an unknown god." Paul discerned a difference between that altar and the idols. It was his ally—a communication key which would probably fit the locks on the minds and hearts of those Stoic and Epicurean philosophers. When they invited him to present his views formally in a setting more conducive to reasoned discussion than the marketplace, Paul was ready.

Paul's venue was a meeting of "The Areopagus," i.e., *The Mars Hill Society*—a group of prominent Athenians who met on Mars Hill to discuss matters of history, philosophy or religion. It was on that same hill, nearly six centuries earlier, that Epimenides once grappled with the problem of pestilence in Athens.

...ul could have launched his Mars Hill address simply by calling a spade a spade. He could have said, "Men of Athens, with all your fine philosophies you still condone idolatry if not actually practice it! Repent or perish!" And every word might well have been true!

Further, he would have been trying to "turn them from darkness to light," as Jesus commanded. But it would have been like a batter hitting the ball and running straight to second base. One must touch first base first! That is why Jesus included the command "open their eyes" as a prerequisite for turning people from "darkness to light."

Paul "ran for first" with the following words: "Men of Athens! I see that in every way you are very religious [remarkable restraint, considering how much Paul loathed idolatry]. For as I walked around and observed your objects of worship [some with Paul's background might have preferred to call them 'filthy idols'], I even found an altar with this inscription: TO AN UNKNOWN GOD."

Then Paul voiced a pronouncement that had waited six centuries for utterance: "Now what you worship as something unknown I am going to proclaim to you" (Acts 17:22-23). Was the God whom Paul proclaimed really a *foreign* god as the philosophers surmised? Not at all! By Paul's reasoning, *Yahweh*, the Judeo-Christian God, was anticipated by Epimenides's altar. He was therefore a God who had already intervened in the history of Athens. Surely He had a right to have His name proclaimed there!

But did Paul really understand the historical background of that altar and the concept of an unknown god? There is evidence that he did! For Epimenides, in addition to his ability to shed light upon murky problems of man/god relationships, was also a *poet*!

And Paul quoted Epimenides's poetry! Leaving a missionary named Titus to strengthen churches on the island of Crete, Paul later wrote instructions to guide Titus in his dealings with Cretans: "Even one of their own prophets has said, 'Cretans are always liars, evil brutes, lazy gluttons.' This testimony is true. Therefore, rebuke them sharply, so that they will be sound in the faith" (Titus 1:12-13).

The words Paul quoted are from a poem ascribed to Epimenides.[5] Notice also that Paul called Epimenides "a prophet." The Greek word is *propheetees*, the same word Paul commonly used to refer to both Old and New Testament prophets. Surely Paul would not have honored Epimenides with the title of prophet apart from knowledge of Epimenides's character and deeds! A man whom Paul could quote as rebuking others for certain evil traits was, by implication, judged by Paul as not noticeably guilty of those traits himself!

Further, in his Mars Hill address Paul states that God has "made every nation of men . . . so that men would seek him and perhaps reach out for him and find him, though he is not far from each one of us" (Acts 17:26-27). These words may constitute an oblique reference to Epimenides as an example of a pagan man who "reached out and found" a God who, though unknown by name, was in reality not far away!

Presumably members of the Mars Hill Society were also familiar with the story of Epimenides from the writings of Plato, Aristotle and others. They must have listened with admiration as Paul began his address on that perceptive cross-cultural footing. But could this Christian apostle, trained under Gamaliel the Jewish scholar, hold the attention of men weaned on the logic of Plato and Aristotle long enough to get the gospel across to them?

Following his stunning opening remarks, Paul's success in the main part of his address would depend upon one thing. Call it "gapless logic." As long as each successive statement which Paul made followed logically from statements preceding, the philosophers would listen. If he left a gap in his reasoning, the philosophers would cut him off at once! It was a rule of the philosophical training they had received—a discipline they imposed upon themselves and would just as readily require of any stranger who claimed to have propositions worthy of their attention.

Could Paul's gospel presentation pass this severe scrutiny?

For several minutes Paul fared very well indeed. Beginning with the testimony of Epimenides's altar Paul proceeded next to the evidence of creation. Then he moved on from the evidence of creation to the inconsistency of idolatry. By then he had worked his way to a position where he could even identify Athenian idolatry as "ignorance" without losing his audience. He went on to say, "[*Theos*] now . . . commands all people everywhere to repent. For he has set a day when he will judge the world with justice by the man he has appointed" (Acts 17:30-31).

In other words, having found and used an "eye-opener" to get to "first base," Paul was "heading for second" in obedience to Jesus' second command—he was seeking to turn the Athenians "from darkness to light!" Then he went on to say: "He has given proof of this to all men by raising him from the dead."

And here—for the first time—Paul left a gap in the logic of his Mars Hill address. He mentioned the resurrection of the man God authorized to judge the world *without first explaining how and why He had to die in the first place*.

The philosophers pounced at once—to their own spiritual impoverishment. "When they heard about the resurrection of the dead, some of them sneered, but others said, 'We want to hear you again on this subject.' At that, Paul left the Council" (Acts 17:32-33).

Paul had already exposed their inconsistency in tolerating, if not actually abetting, idolatry. That alone was no small accomplishment among a panel of men who prided themselves for rational consistency! As seekers of truth they should have followed through with Paul on the implications of at least his opening remarks, instead of faulting him for a subsequent technicality.

Not all, however, discredited Paul for his mention of the resurrection: "A few men became followers of Paul and believed. Among them was Dionysius, a member of the Areopagus" (Acts 17:34). Second-century tradition says that Dionysius later became the first bishop of Athens! His name is derived from that of Dionysus—a Greek god whose theology included a death-resurrection concept! Could there be a connection between that concept and Dionysius's personal response to a man who so boldly championed a teaching of resurrection?

Later the apostle John, continuing Paul's approach to the Greek philosophical mind, appropriated a favorite Stoic philosophical term— the *Logos*—as a title for Jesus Christ. A Greek philosopher named Heraclitus first used the term *Logos* around 600 B.C. to designate the divine reason or plan which coordinates a changing universe. *Logos* means simply "word." Jews, for their part, emphasized the *memra* (Aramaic for "word") of the Lord. John saw the Greek *logos* and the Jewish *memra* as describing essentially the same valid theological truth. He represented Jesus Christ as the fulfillment of both when he wrote, "In the beginning was the [*Logos*], and the [*Logos*] was with [*Theos*], and the [*Logos*] was [*Theos*]. . . . The [*Logos*] became flesh, and lived for a while among us" (John 1:1,14).

With this vital juxtaposition of both Greek terms—*Theos* and *Logos*—in relation to *Elohim* and to Jesus Christ, Christianity presented itself as *fulfilling* rather than *destroying* something valid in Greek philosophy!

In fact, such terms and concepts were clearly regarded by Christian emissaries to the Greeks as ordained by God to prepare the Greek mind for the gospel! They found these fortuitous Greek philosophical terms to be just as valid as Old Testament messianic metaphors such as "Lamb of God" and "The Lion of the Tribe of Judah." And they used *both sets of terminology with equal freedom* to set the Person of Jesus Christ within the context of both Jewish and Greek culture, respectively.

THE CANAANITES

Actually, New Testament apostles like Paul and John were not the first to use the above strategy for making God's identity clear to pagans. No less important a figure than Abraham used the same method two thousand years earlier! Here is the story.

"Yahweh"—"God" in our language—gave a man initially called Abram some awesome promises about 4,000 years ago. Yahweh had told Abram to leave his own country, his own people, and his own father's household, and migrate to a very distant and presumably benighted foreign country (see Gen. 12:1). If Abram (whose name was later changed to *Abraham*) would obey this command, Yahweh promised the following: "I will make you into a great nation and I will bless you; I will make your name great, and you will be a blessing. I will bless those who bless you, and whoever curses you I will curse" (Gen. 12:2-3).

Up to this point, Yahweh's special arrangement with Abram does not sound very different from multitudes of similar pacts which tribal gods throughout history have made with their own exclusive little circles of devotees in various parts of planet Earth. Was Yahweh, as some critics have insinuated, just another petty tribal god whetting the self-interest of a follower with grandiose promises designed to keep him coming back again and again with more and more worship and homage?

That insinuation might have been hard to counter, were it not for the bottom line of this Yahweh-Abram agreement. For Yahweh went on to say, "And *all peoples on Earth will be blessed through you*" (Gen. 12:3, emphasis added).

And that statement lets a special characteristic of Yahweh's promises shine through! He was not blessing Abram to make him egotistical, arrogant, aloof, or self-centered. Yahweh blessed him to make him a blessing—and not just to his own kin! This blessing is targeted toward nothing less than all peoples on Earth! And nothing could be less selfish or less provincial!

Theologians call this set of promises the *Abrahamic Covenant*, but it is far more than just a covenant between God and one particular man. It marked the beginning of a startling new development in something theologians call *special revelation*! In other words, by the time Yahweh had fulfilled all His promises to Abram, mankind would be able to fathom the wisdom, love and power of Yahweh in ways that previously were inconceivable, not merely to men, but apparently even to angels as well (see 1 Pet. 1:12).

To launch Abram on his way toward his new destiny as "a blessing to all peoples," Yahweh first led him to a foreign region inhabited by an entire spectrum of tribes, each of which in turn encompassed many clans and families. These tribes were the Canaanites, Kenites, Kenizzites, Kadmonites, Hittites, Perizzites, Rephaites, Amorites, Girgashites and Jebusites (see Gen. 15:19). In addition to these 10, approximately 30 other entire peoples spreading from Egypt to Chaldea are mentioned *by name* in the first 36 chapters of Genesis alone. More ethnic subdivisions of mankind are given specific recognition in these 36 chapters than in any other section of comparable length anywhere else in the Bible!

Driving in the slow lane among so many ethnic groups, Abram was more than likely to develop the kind of *all-peoples perspective* that would surely be required in one destined to be a "blessing to all peoples"!

Everything, it seemed, was proceeding just as Abram should have expected. But Yahweh had a surprise in store for him . . .

When Yahweh said, "All peoples on Earth will be blessed through you," Abram probably thought Yahweh meant that he and the nation yet to spring from him would become the *sole* source of spiritual illumination for all of mankind. But that was not exactly what Yahweh had in mind!

To be sure, when Abram finally approached Canaan (as that foreign land proved to be called), he soon learned that at least two of Canaan's cities— Sodom and Gomorrah—were already steeped in utter decadence. Others, particularly cities of the Amorites, were beginning to follow Sodom and Gomorrah's example (see. Gen. 15:16). It looked as if Yahweh, the Almighty, had no advocate other than Abram in that entire region of the world, which must have made Abram feel very needed!

When, however, Abram and his caravan traveled deeper into Canaan, a delightful surprise awaited them. They passed near a city which took its name from the Canaanite word for "peace"—*Salem*. The Canaanite name of that very city, incidentally, would later give rise to the very meaningful Hebrew greeting *Shalom* and also its Arabic equivalent *Salaam*. *Salem* would later contribute its five letters to form the last part of the name Jeru*salem*—"the foundation of peace." Even more interesting than Salem itself, however, was the king who reigned over it— Melchizedek!

His name is a combination of two other Canaanite words: *melchi*— "king," and *zadok*—"righteousness."

A "king of righteousness" among the Canaanites, who were notorious for idolatry, child sacrifice, legalized homosexuality and temple prostitution? Surely Melchizedek must have been grossly misnamed!

Not so! A few years later Abram, returning from an amazing rescue operation against Kedorlaomer (see Gen. 14:1-16), came to a valley called, in the Canaanite language, *Shaveh*. Canaanites in those days customarily designated Shaveh valley as "the valley of the king" (see Gen. 14:17). *Which* king?

It is not hard to guess! A Jewish historian named Josephus tells us that the Valley of Shaveh was none other than the Hinnom valley—just

below the southern wall of what is now old Jerusalem! Modern archaeologists, excavating the ruins of the Jerusalem of David's time, expect
soon to uncover the ruins of an ancient Canaanite town on that same
slope between the Valley of Shaveh and the south wall of old Jerusalem!

It would not at all be surprising if those long buried ruins turn out
to be Melchizedek's city—the original Salem. And the Valley of Shaveh—
the "valley of the king" was very likely so named in honor of King
Melchizedek himself!

Abram had no sooner arrived in this "valley of the king" when King
Melchizedek himself "brought out bread and wine" for Abram's refresh-
ment. The narrator does not say that Melchizedek "journeyed to meet
Abram, bearing bread and wine," but that he simply "brought out bread
and wine"—perhaps another evidence for the close proximity of the
Valley of Shaveh and Salem.

Now comes the unexpected. This Canaanite "king of righteousness,"
according to the author of Genesis doubled also as "priest of [*El
Elyon*]"—"God Most High" (Gen. 14:18). Who was *El Elyon*?

Both *El* and *Elyon* were Canaanite names for Yahweh Himself. *El*
occurs frequently in ancient Ugaritic texts.[6] This Canaanite name *El* even
worked its way into the Hebrew language of Abram's descendants in
such words as Beth*el*—"the house of God," *El Shaddai*—"God Almighty,"
and *El*ohim—"God" (a pluralized form of *El* which nevertheless retains a
mysteriously singular meaning).

Elyon likewise shows up as a name for God in ancient texts written
in Phoenician—a later branch of Melchizedek's old Canaanite language.[7]
And even the compound form *El Elyon* appears in an ancient Aramaic
inscription found recently in Syria.[8] Compounded together, the two
terms *El* and *Elyon* mean "God most High."

Question: Did Abram the Chaldean, who apparently called the
Almighty *Yahweh*, balk at Melchizedek's use of this Canaanite term *El
Elyon* as a valid name for God? We do not have to wait for an answer!
Melchizedek did something which put Abram's attitude to the test
immediately: "[Melchizedek] blessed Abram, saying, 'Blessed be Abram
by El Elyon, Creator of heaven and Earth. And blessed be El Elyon, who
delivered [Abram's] enemies into [his] hand'" (Gen. 14:19-20).

Brace yourself for Abram's reply. We may be about to listen in on the first theological argument in the biblical narrative. What will Abram say? Will he reply, "One moment, your highness! The correct name for the Almighty is *Yahweh*, not *El Elyon*! Furthermore, I cannot possibly accept a blessing offered under this Canaanite name *El Elyon*, since any Canaanite concept of the Almighty undoubtedly must be tainted with pagan notions. In any case, Yahweh has told me that *I* am the one who is supposed to be a blessing to all peoples on Earth, including Canaanites like you. Don't you think you have been a little presumptuous in blessing me?"

No! Abram's response was simply to give Melchizedek "a tenth of everything" he had recovered from Kedorlaomer in the rescue operation (see Gen. 14:20). This action by Abram in thus "paying the tithe" to Melchizedek later triggered an extensive commentary by the New Testament author of the Epistle to the Hebrews. For example: "Just think how great [Melchizedek] was: Even the patriarch Abraham gave him a tenth of the plunder!" The writer went on to argue that Canaanite Melchizedek's priesthood must on this basis be considered superior to the Hebrew people's own Levitical priesthood, on the ground that "Levi . . . paid the tenth [to Melchizedek] through Abraham, because when Melchizedek met Abraham, Levi was still in the body of his ancestor [Abraham]" (Heb. 7:4-10).

Concerning Melchizedek's action in blessing Abraham, and Abraham's implied acceptance of that blessing, the same author comments that Melchizedek "blessed him who had *the promises*. And without doubt the lesser person is blessed by the greater" (Heb. 7:6-7, emphasis added).

But that is not all that points to the incredible greatness of this Canaanite personage called Melchizedek. The author of Hebrews then quotes a prophecy by the Hebrew King David—the king who first wrested Melchizedek's ancient Salem from the Jebusites (1000 B.C.) and made it Jerusalem, capital of the Hebrew nation. David's prophecy explicitly states that the Jewish Messiah, when He comes, will not serve as a member of the inherently temporary Levitical priesthood with its restricted lineage. Rather, He will be a priest of "the order of Melchizedek," in which membership is apparently not restricted to one particular lineage.

Not only that, but Messiah's membership in this "order of Melchizedek" is confirmed by nothing less than a divine oath; and His membership in Melchizedek's order is eternal! "The Lord has *sworn*, and will not change his mind: 'You are a *priest forever*, in the order of Melchizedek'" (Ps. 110:4, emphasis added).

Perhaps Yahweh warned Abram in advance that he would find someone like Melchizedek already standing up for the true God among the Canaanites. All I can say is, if Yahweh *didn't* tell Abram beforehand about Melchizedek (and the record gives no clue that He did), then the discovery of a man like Melchizedek among those "benighted Canaanites" must have really rocked father Abram back on his heels!

How can we make sense of the biblical claim that Melchizedek was greater in spiritual rank than Abraham? What was it that made Melchizedek greater?

It seems to this writer that the answer lies in what Melchizedek *represented* vis-à-vis what Abraham represented in God's economy. The thesis of this book is that Melchizedek stood in the Valley of Shaveh as a figurehead, or type, of God's *general* revelation to mankind, and that Abraham correspondingly represented God's covenant-based, canon-recorded *special* revelation to mankind. God's general revelation is greater than His special revelation in the following two ways: it is *older*, and it influences 100 percent of mankind (see Ps. 19) instead of just a small percentage! Thus it was fitting that Abraham, as the representative of a younger, less universal kind of revelation should pay his tithe of acknowledgment to the representative of general revelation.

Not that Melchizedek's prior presence in Canaan detracted in any way from Abraham's special God-given destiny! On the contrary, there is not the slightest evidence that these two men regarded each other with even a hint of jealousy or competition. Melchizedek shared his "bread and wine" with Abraham and blessed him, and Abraham "paid the tithe" to Melchizedek. They were brothers in *El Elyon/Yahweh* and allies in His cause! Since general revelation and special revelation both spring from *El Elyon/Yahweh*, it was to be expected that Melchizedek would share bread and wine with Abram and that Abram would "pay the tithe" to Melchizedek.

The amazing thing is that they have continued to do just that down through the subsequent history of mankind. For as Yahweh's special revelation—let's call it the *Abraham factor*—has continued to reach out into the world through both the Old and New Testament eras, it has continually found that Yahweh's general revelation—let's call it the *Melchizedek factor*—is already on the scene, bringing out the bread, the wine and the blessing of welcome!

Eternity in Their Hearts is my attempt to trace through history some examples of this beautiful interaction between the Melchizedek factor—God's general revelation—and the Abraham factor—God's special revelation.

But a third factor exists as well. And its relationship is not beautiful. Still another Canaanite king, one of very different character from Melchizedek, met Abram that same day in the Valley of Shaveh. Bera, king of Sodom.

Bera, too, was friendly to Abram. He offered to let Abram keep the spoil Abram had retrieved from Kedorlaomer—spoil which came originally from Sodom.

Observe Abram's reaction: "Abram said to the king of Sodom, 'I have raised my hand to the Lord God Most High [*Yahweh—El Elyon* in the original. Just as the apostles Paul and John later accepted Plato's *Theos* and *Logos* as valid Greek names for the True God, so also Abraham in his day accepted *El Elyon*, Melchizedek's Canaanite name for God as valid], Creator of heaven and Earth, and have taken an oath that I will accept nothing belonging to you, not even a thread or the thong of a sandal, so that you will never be able to say, "I have made Abram rich"'" (Gen. 14:22-23).

Representatives of the Abraham factor down through history have had to follow Abram's example in exercising this same discernment—the discernment that can distinguish the truly friendly Melchizedek factor among the Canaanites from that other occultish component of Canaanite culture—let's call it the *Sodom factor*. They have had to learn to respond to the one and reject the other, just as Abram did in the Valley of Shaveh.

Now for our next example of these *three* factors intermingling and/or reacting in history:

THE INCAS

Question: If God gave *two* pagan peoples—Canaanites and Greeks—prior witness of His existence, could He not also have extended the same or at least a similar providence to other pagan peoples as well? Perhaps even to *all* of them?

In other words, has the God who prepared the gospel for all peoples also prepared all peoples for the gospel? If He has, then the current assumption, held by millions of believers and nonbelievers alike, that pagan people cannot understand and generally do not want to receive the Christian gospel, and that it is therefore unfair (and almost more work than it is worth) to try to get them to accept it, must be a false assumption.

In the rest of this book, I will prove that this assumption is false. God has indeed prepared the Gentile world to receive the gospel. Significant numbers of non-Christians, therefore, have proved them-selves many times more willing to receive the gospel than we Christians historically have been to share it with them. Read on—

The apostle Paul called Epimenides a "prophet." One wonders what title he would have ascribed to Pachacuti, whose spiritual insight as a pagan far surpassed even Epimenides's.

Pachacuti (sometimes spelled *Pachacutec*) ruled as king of South America's incredible Inca civilization from A.D. 1438 to 1471.[9] According to Philip Ainsworth Means, late authority on Andean antiquities, it was Pachacuti who brought the Inca Empire to its finest flowering.[10] What were some of his accomplishments? Well, to begin with, when Pachacuti rebuilt Cuzco, the Inca capital, he worked on a grand scale indeed, replete with palaces, forts and a refurbished temple to the sun. Then he added a "fabulous golden precinct" at Coricancha—a building of "magnificence rivaling even Solomon's Temple in Jerusalem!"[11] He also constructed a long line of fortresses protecting eastern frontiers of his empire from invasion by tribes of the Amazon basin. One such fortress, majestic Machu Picchu (portrayed on the cover of this book), became for a time a last refuge of the Incan upper class in its flight from Spain's brutal conquistadores. In fact, the conquistadores never found

Machu Picchu. Pachacuti built it on a soaring mountain ridge, rendering it invisible from lower elevations.

For several centuries, knowledge of Machu Picchu's existence was lost to the outside world. Thick jungle overwhelmed the site. Then, in 1904, an engineer named Franklin caught a glimpse of the ruins from a distant mountain. Franklin told Thomas Paine about the site. Paine, an English missionary, was serving under a society called Regions Beyond Missionary Union. In 1906 Paine climbed to the ruins with another missionary, Stuart McNairn. They stood in awe. Not until 1910 did Yale's Hiram Bingham, hearing of the discovery, visit Paine at Urco. Paine kindly outfitted Bingham with mules and guides for a journey to the site. Bingham thereafter made himself world famous as "discoverer of Machu Picchu, Lost City of the Incas"! Bingham chose not to give a single byline of credit to Thomas Paine, mentioning only "local rumor" as the factor which guided him.[12]

Medical doctor Daniel Hayden, who knew Thomas Paine personally over a period of years in Peru, affirms that Paine—a humble man beloved by Inca descendants throughout Peru—chose not to try to correct Hiram Bingham's "oversight." Thomas Paine remains just one of innumerable Christian missionaries whose contributions to science have been denied recognition by men of science.

Millions of tourists have visited Machu Picchu since Peru's new Hiram Bingham Highway made it accessible in 1948. Anyone who has been awed by the splendor of Machu Picchu should know that Pachacuti, the king who apparently founded it, is credited with an achievement far more significant than merely building fortresses, cities, temples or monuments. Like Epimenides, Pachacuti was one of those spiritual explorers who, in the words of Paul (see Acts 17:27), sought, reached out for and found a God far greater than any popular "god" of his own culture. Unlike Epimenides, however, Pachacuti did not leave the God of his discovery in the category of "unknown." He identified that God by name, and more.

Almost everyone who knows anything about Incas knows that they deified Inti—the sun.

Yet in 1575, in Cuzco, a Spanish priest named Cristobel de Molina collected a number of Inca hymns—and certain traditions associated with them—which prove that the deity of Inti was not always left unquestioned by Incas themselves. De Molina wrote the hymns and their associated traditions in the Inca language, called Quechua, with orthography adapted from Spanish. The Incas themselves had no writing system. That entire collection of traditions and hymns trace back to the reign of Pachacuti.

Modern scholars, rediscovering de Molina's collection, marveled at their revolutionary content. Some at first refused to believe they were genuinely Inca! Surely, they thought, de Molina himself must have edited his own European thought into the original Inca composition. Alfred Metraux, however, in his *History of the Incas*, agrees with Professor John H. Rowe who, he says, "has succeeded in restoring the hymns to their original version, [and is] convinced that they owe nothing to the missionaries' teaching. The forms and expressions used are basically different to those of the Christian liturgy in the Inca tongue."[13]

Further confirmation of the authenticity of de Molina's compilation has surfaced. Still another hymn of the same genre, Metraux says, was "miraculously preserved by Yamqui Salcamaygua Pachacuti, a 17-century Indian chronicler. . . . One has only to compare [this other hymn with those] collected by de Molina in 1575 to realize that they all belong to the same literary and religious traditions."[14]

Metraux states: "For profundity of thought and soaring lyricism [the Inca hymn preserved by Yamqui] can bear comparison with the loveliest of the Psalms."[15]

What was so revolutionary about the hymns? The traditions discovered with them state bluntly that Pachacuti—the king so committed to sun worship that he rebuilt Inti's temple at Cuzco—later began to question his god's credentials! Philip Ainsworth Means, commenting on Pachacuti's discontent with Inti, wrote: "He pointed out how that luminary always follows a set path, performs definite tasks, and keeps certain hours as does a laborer." In other words, if Inti is God, why doesn't he ever do anything *original*? The king mused again. He noted, "the solar radiance can be dimmed by any passing cloud." In other words, if Inti were truly God, *no mere created thing could dim his light!*[16]

Suddenly Pachacuti tumbled to the realization that he had been worshiping a mere thing as Creator! Bravely he advanced to the inevitable next question: If Inti is not the true God, *then who is?*

Where could a pagan Inca, cut off from Judeo-Christian illumination, find an answer to a question like that?

The answer is quite simple—from old traditions lying dormant within his own culture! That such an event is possible was foreseen by none other than the apostle Paul when he wrote that Theos, in the past, "let all nations go their own way. Yet *he has not left himself without testimony*" (Acts 14:16-17, emphasis added).

Pachacuti took the testimony he himself had derived directly from creation and aligned it with his own culture's almost extinct memory of *Viracocha*—the Lord, the omnipotent Creator of all things.

All that remained of earlier Incan allegiance to *Viracocha* was a shrine called *Quishuarcancha*, located in the upper Vilcañota Valley.[17] Pachacuti recalled also that his own father, Hatun Tupac, once claimed to receive counsel in a dream from *Viracocha*. Viracocha reminded Hatun Tupac in that dream that He was truly the *Creator of all things*. Hatun Tupac promptly renamed himself (dare we say presumptuously?) Viracocha!

The concept of Viracocha, therefore, was probably of great antiquity. Worship of Inti and other gods, in this view, were only recent departures from a purer original belief system. Metraux implies as much when he observes that Viracocha-like figures are prominent in Indian cultures "from Alaska to Tierra del Fuego,"[18] whereas sun worship appears in relatively few cultures.

Pachacuti apparently decided that his father had rediscovered something basic and genuine, but had simply not taken the discovery as far as it deserved to go! He resolved that he, as his father's son, would take the reality his father had touched to greater lengths (or was it in fact that reality which was taking him to greater lengths?).

A God who created all things, Pachacuti concluded, deserves worship! And it would be inconsistent at the same time to worship part of His creation as if it were Him! Pachacuti came to a brisk decision—this Inti-as-God nonsense had been around long enough, at least as far as he and his upper-class subjects were concerned.

Pachacuti took action. He called a congress of the priests of the sun—a pagan equivalent of the Nicene Council if you like—at beautiful Coricancha. In fact, one scholar dubs that congress the *Council of Coricancha*, thus ranking it among the great theological councils of history.[19] In that council Pachacuti presented his doubts about Inti in "the three sentences":

1. Inti cannot be universal if, while giving light to some, he withholds it from others.
2. He cannot be perfect if he can never remain at ease, resting.
3. Nor can he be all-powerful when the smallest cloud may cover him.[20]

Pachacuti then revived his upper-class subjects' faint memory of omnipotent *Viracocha* by listing his awesome attributes. Dr. B. C. Brundage of the University of Oklahoma summarizes Pachacuti's description of *Viracocha* as follows:

He is ancient, remote, supreme, and uncreated. Nor does he need the gross satisfaction of a consort. He manifests himself as a trinity when he wishes, . . . otherwise only heavenly warriors and archangels surround his loneliness. He created all peoples by his "word" [shades of Heraclitus, Plato, Philo and the apostle John!], as well as all huacas [spirits]. He is man's Fortunus, ordaining his years and nourishing him. He is indeed the very principle of life, for he warms the folk through his created son, Punchao [the sun disk, which was somehow distinct from Inti]. He is a bringer of peace and an orderer. He is in his own being blessed and has pity on men's wretchedness. He alone judges and absolves them and enables them to combat their evil tendencies.[21]

Pachacuti then commanded that Inti from that time forward be respected as a "kinsman" only—a fellow created entity. Prayer was to be directed to Viracocha with the deepest awe and humility.[22]

In the aftermath of the council, Pachacuti composed reverent hymns to *Viracocha*, hymns which eventually found their way into de Molina's collection.

Some priests of the sun reacted with "bitter hostility."[23] Pachacuti's statements hit their vested interests like bombshells. Others found Pachacuti's logic irresistible and agreed to give allegiance to *Viracocha*! Of these, many were troubled, however, by one very practical problem: How would the masses react when priests of the sun announced, "Everything our priesthood has taught these past few centuries has been wrong! Inti is not God after all! These immense temples you built for him with awesome toil—and by our command—are vain. All rituals and prayers connected with Inti are futile. Now we must begin again at ground zero with the true God—*Viracocha*!"

Might not such an announcement arouse cynicism? Or even trigger social upheaval?

Pachacuti bowed to political expediency. "He ordained . . . that the worship of Viracocha be confined to the ruling caste, [for it was] . . . too subtle and sublime for ordinary folk [sic!]."[24]

To be fair, Pachacuti may have hoped that the worship of *Viracocha*—given time to permeate like leaven—might eventually work its way down to the lower classes. Time, however, was something his budding reformation did not have much of. Pachacuti little dreamed how fateful his decision to favor upper classes was. Upper classes, historically, are a notoriously short-lived social phenomenon; it is the common people who endure. So it proved also with the Inca upper class. Within a century of Pachacuti's death, merciless Spanish conquistadores obliterated both the royal family and the upper class. Since the lower classes had been relegated to spiritual darkness with their mistaken notions about Inti and other fictional gods, they were incapable of carrying on Pachacuti's reformation. Thus it died in infancy, a mini reformation.

Why did the Inca Empire topple within a mere century of its zenith under King Pachacuti? Was *Viracocha* angry because the upper class hoarded the knowledge of His person from common people? And what would have happened if Christian missionaries from Europe had reached Peru two or three generations ahead of the conquistadores?

Surely that period was the optimum time for the gospel to arrive. Interest in the concept of one supreme God was at a fever pitch in the royal family and the upper class. Bearers of the gospel would have had nearly a century to reap a glorious spiritual harvest throughout the empire before the conquistadores struck! Incas themselves, moreover, believed a vague prophecy that one day, *Viracocha* would bring them blessing from the west, i.e., by sea. But compassionate Christian message-bearers, whoever they should have been, defaulted. In their place came a heartless political conqueror and commercialist—Pizarro—and his rapacious army. Pretending that he was acting in God's name, Pizarro approached Peru by sea and exploited Incan monotheistic expectations to destroy both the Incas and their empire.

Even before Pizarro, Hernando Cortez exploited similar expectations among the Aztecs and destroyed them. How differently history might have unfolded if only true messengers of the gospel had arrived first! Not only to deliver their message, but also to serve Aztecs, Incas and other endangered peoples of the Americas as ombudsmen, teaching them in advance how to deal with ruthless political/commercial forces soon to follow. Aztecs and Incas would then not have bowed to Cortez and Pizarro as fulfillers of their legends, since the legends would already have been fulfilled! Maya, Aztec and Inca empires might have survived to this day.

And how ironic that Spanish Catholics, in their zeal to abolish Inca "idolatry," destroyed a monotheistic belief which, in effect, constituted an interim Old Testament to open the minds of thousands to the good news of *Viracocha*'s incarnation in the Person of His Son. Notice that I said "interim" Old Testament, not "substitute" Old Testament.

Omar Khayyam's "moving hand," however, "writes, and having writ, moves on." It is too late now to bring back Pachacuti and his empire that we might deal with them more justly than did the Spaniards. What matters now? That we, children of this present generation, deal fairly with Pachacuti's children who survived the Spanish holocaust—the Quechuas.

Let's place Pachacuti's reformation in historical perspective. Compare him for a moment with Akhenaten, an Egyptian pharaoh who also attempted religious reform. Egyptologists acclaim Akhenaten (1379 to 1361 B.C.) as a rare genius because he attempted—unsuccessfully—to replace the grossly confused idolatry of ancient Egypt with sun worship.[25] Yet Pachacuti stands leagues ahead of Akhenaten for his realization that the sun, which could merely blind human eyes, was no match for a God too great to be seen by human eyes! How strange then that modern scholars have widely publicized Akhenaten's reform while mentioning Pachacuti's reform only in obscure textbooks for the initiated.

Let's set the record straight.

If Akhenaten's sun worship was a step above idolatry, Pachacuti's choice of God above sun worship was a leap into the stratosphere! Discovering a man like Pachacuti in fifteenth-century Peru is as startling as finding an Abraham in Ur or a Melchizedek among the Canaanites! If only it were possible to travel back in time, Pachacuti is one man I would certainly like to look in on. I like to call him the "Incan Melchizedek."

Both the Athenians and Cretans of Epimenides's time and the Incas of Pachacuti's day died without hearing the gospel of Jesus Christ. How about it? Are there no God-anticipating pagan peoples who *did* live to receive the blessing of the gospel?

History does indeed record many such. Here is one . . .

THE SANTAL

In 1867, a bearded Norwegian missionary named Lars Skrefsrud and his Danish colleague, a layman named Hans Børreson, found two-and-a-half million people called the Santal living in a region north of Calcutta, India. Skrefsrud soon proved himself an amazing linguist. He quickly became so fluent in Santal that people came from miles around just to hear a foreigner speak their language so well!

As soon as possible, Skrefsrud began proclaiming the gospel to the Santal. Naturally he wondered how many years it would take before Santal people, until then so far removed from Jewish or Christian influences, would even show interest in the gospel, let alone open their hearts to it.

To Skrefsrud's utter amazement, the Santal were electrified almost at once by the gospel message. At length he heard Santal sages, including one named Kolean, exclaim, "What this stranger is saying must mean that Thakur Jiu has not forgotten us after all this time!"

Skrefsrud caught his breath in astonishment. *Thakur* was a Santal word meaning "genuine." *Jiu* meant "god."

The Genuine God?

Clearly, Skrefsrud was not introducing a new concept by talking about one supreme God. Santal sages politely brushed aside the terminology he had been using for God and insisted that *Thakur Jiu* was the right name to use. That name, obviously, had been on Santal lips for a very long time!

"How do you know about *Thakur Jiu?*" Skrefsrud asked (a little disappointed, perhaps).

"Our forefathers knew Him long ago," the Santal replied, beaming.

"Very well," Skrefsrud continued, "I have a second question. Since you know about *Thakur Jiu*, why don't you worship Him instead of the sun, or worse yet, demons?"

Santal faces around him grew wistful. "That," they responded, "is the *bad* news." Then the Santal sage named Kolean stepped forward and said, "Let me tell you our story from the very beginning."

Not only Skrefsrud, but also the entire gathering of younger Santal, fell silent as Kolean, an esteemed elder, spun out a story that stirred the dust on aeons of Santal oral tradition . . .

Long, long ago, according to Kolean, *Thakur Jiu*—the Genuine God—created the first man— Haram—and the first woman—Ayo—and placed them far to the west of India in a region called Hihiri Pipiri. There a being named Lita tempted them to make rice beer. Then Lita enticed them to pour part of the beer on the ground as an offering to Satan. Haram and Ayo became drunk on the rest of the beer and slept. When they awoke, they knew they were naked and felt ashamed.

Skrefsrud marveled at the biblical parallel in Kolean's story.

But there was more . . .

Ayo later bore Haram seven sons and seven daughters, who married and founded seven clans. The clans migrated to a region called Kroj Kaman, where they became corrupted. *Thakur Jiu* called mankind to "return to Him." When man refused, *Thakur Jiu* hid "a holy pair" in a cave on Mount Harata (note the resemblance to the biblical name "Ararat"). Then *Thakur Jiu* destroyed the rest of mankind with a flood. Later, descendants of the "holy pair" multiplied and migrated to a plain called Sasan Beda ("mustard field"). There *Thakur Jiu* divided them into many different peoples.

A branch of mankind (which we shall call "proto-Santal") migrated first to "Jarpi land," and then continued eastward "from forest to forest" until high mountains blocked their way. Desperately they sought a way through the mountains, but every route proved impassable, at least to their women and children. Not unlike the children of Israel in Sinai, the people became faint on their journey.

In those days, Kolean explained, the proto-Santal, as descendants of the holy pair, still acknowledged Thakur Jiu as the genuine God. Facing this crisis, however, they lost their faith in Him and took their first step into spiritism. "The spirits of these great mountains have blocked our way," they decided. "Come, let us bind ourselves to them by an oath, so that they will let us pass." Then they covenanted with the *Maran Buru* (spirits of the great mountains), saying, "O, *Maran Buru*, if you release the pathways for us, we will practice spirit appeasement when we reach the other side."

Skrefsrud no doubt had thought it strange that the Santal name for wicked spirits meant literally "spirits of the great mountains," especially since there were no great mountains in the present Santal homeland. Now he understood.

"Very shortly," Kolean continued, "they came upon a passage [the Khyber Pass?] in the direction of the rising sun." They named that passage *Bain*, which means "day gate." Thus the proto-Santal burst through onto the plains of what is now called Pakistan and India. Subsequent migrations brought them still further east to the border regions between India and the present Bangladesh, where they became the modern Santal people.[26]

Under bondage to their oath, and not out of love for the *Maran Buru*, the Santal began to practice spirit appeasement, sorcery and even sun worship. Kolean added: "In the beginning, we did not have gods. The ancient ancestors obeyed *Thakur* only. After finding other gods, day by day we forgot *Thakur* more and more until only His name remained.

"In this present age it is said by some," Kolean continued, "that the sun god is *Thakur*. Therefore, when there are religious ceremonies . . . [some people] look up to the sun . . . and speak unto *Thakur*. But the forefathers taught us that *Thakur* is distinct. He is not to be seen with fleshly eyes, but he sees all. He has created all things. He has set everything in its place, and he nourishes all, great and small."[27]

How did Skrefsrud respond? Some missionaries, to be sure, have responded in similar situations by saying, "Forget this being you think is God! He can only be the devil! I will tell you who the true God is." Such arrogant reactions have often quashed the potential responsiveness of entire peoples.

Skrefsrud was not of that breed. Just as Abraham freely accepted *El Elyon*, Melchizedek's Canaanite name for God, and just as Paul, Barnabas, John and their successors followed a path blazed by Greek philosophers when they accepted the Greek names *Logos* and *Theos* as valid names for the Almighty, so Lars decided to learn a lesson from Kolean and his forefathers. He accepted *Thakur Jiu* as Yahweh's name among the Santal.

Skrefsrud found no disqualifying barnacles of error attached to the name *Thakur Jiu*. It was not in the *Zeus* category, worthy of rejection, but in the *Theos/Logos* category, worthy of acceptance. Further, he reasoned that if he as a Norwegian could call the Almighty *Gud*—a name which sprang from just as pagan a background as *Theos* in Greek and *Deus* in Latin—then surely Santal had a right to call Him *Thakur Jiu*!

Skrefsrud accepted the name! For a while, to be sure, it felt strange to hear his own lips proclaiming Jesus Christ as the Son of *Thakur Jiu*! But only for a couple of weeks. After that, the strangeness wore off. No doubt it sounded just as strange the first time someone said that Jesus Christ was the Son of *Theos*, or of *Deus*, or of *Gud* or, for that matter, of *God*!

Did Skrefsrud's acceptance of the Santal name for God make any difference? Doesn't a rose by any other name smell just as sweet? In a garden, yes! But not in the memory! The very word "rose" has power to evoke fond reminiscence of color and scent. Substituting the word "thistle" will not change the rose, but it will cut off the hearer's fond reminiscence. For centuries uncounted, Santal children had grown up hearing their parents exclaim in their gardens or around cooking fires: "Oh, if only our forefathers hadn't made that grievous mistake we would still know *Thakur Jiu* today! But as things stand, we've lost contact with him. He's probably written us off as an unworthy people and won't have anything more to do with us because our forefathers turned their backs on him at that long-ago crisis in the mountains!"

Using the familiar *Thakur Jiu* before any Santal audience, therefore, would tend to evoke a thousand wistful memories, rendering the audience generally more contemplative, curious and even responsive.

And that is exactly the effect produced by Skrefsrud's and Børreson's preaching![28] In fact, before Skrefsrud and Børreson realized what was happening, they found themselves with literally thousands of Santal inquirers begging to learn how they could be reconciled to *Thakur Jiu* through Jesus Christ! The possibility that the rift between their race and *Thakur Jiu* could be healed excited them no end!

As the teaching of inquirers led to conversions and baptisms, staid pastors in tradition-bound churches of Europe were soon stunned by reports from India, stating that Skrefsrud and Børreson were averaging, during one period, as many as 80 joyful Santal baptisms per day!

"Something must be wrong!" some European theologues exclaimed, thinking it impossible that "heathen who had lived in darkness" for so long could know enough about God and the way of salvation to be both converted and baptized so early in Skrefsrud and Børreson's mission, and in such large numbers! Even a claim of eight baptisms per day would have boggled the minds of European clerics, most of whom would have considered an average of one baptism per week as proof that the blessing of God was mightily upon their ministry!

Eighty baptisms per day, however, signified that young Santal churches in "Hindu India" were growing more than 500 times as fast as most churches in "Christian Europe"! Christians who had long protested that missions to Asia would only prove futile because Asians were so set in their ways and couldn't understand the gospel in any case were soundly rocked back on their heels. Skrefsrud and Børreson, whenever they returned to Europe to lecture in churches, were constantly hailed as heroes of the faith by thousands of rank and file Christians who, learning of the Santal breakthrough, came from miles around to hear the two men. The result was a general quickening of spiritual life in many churches of Europe. Alternating with such gratifying bursts of public acclaim, committees of frowning clerics met to interrogate Skrefsrud and Børreson respectively. They felt compelled to question the depth of Santal response, thinking perhaps that the astonishing success of Skrefsrud and Børreson among "raw heathen" reflected badly upon their own plodding ministries in "enlightened Europe."

Meanwhile, back on the Santal frontier in India, Santal Christians continued manifesting Christian character and proved their mettle by bravely taking the gospel still further among their own people. Skrefsrud himself counted 15,000 baptisms during his years in India. During that time he also translated much of the Bible into the Santal language, compiled a Santal grammar and dictionary, recorded numerous Santal traditions for posterity, and persuaded the colonial government to pass laws protecting the Santal minority from ruthless exploitation by their Hindu neighbors.

Overwhelmed by the size of the harvest they had triggered, Skrefsrud, Børreson and their wives sent out a cry for help! Other missionaries rushed in to help them reap the fast-ripening Santal harvest, and within a few more decades, still another 85,000 believers were baptized under Skrefsrud's Santal mission alone. By that time, Baptists and other groups had rushed in to stake their claims along the Santal lode, accounting for several tens of thousands more Santal Christians!

The Santal story is just one of hundreds of case histories in which entire peoples of the non-Christian world have demonstrated far greater enthusiasm in receiving the gospel than we Christians have shown for sending it to them.

Kolean's comment to Skrefsrud about Santal sun worshipers mingling Thakur Jiu's name with their sun worship is instructive. Just as the king of Sodom tried to insinuate himself into Abraham's life, so also sun worshipers or idolaters may sometimes try to add prestige to their rituals by associating God's name with them. Practitioners of the occult sometimes do the same with European names for the Almighty, such as *God, Gott* or *Gud*. Researchers who investigate only the cultic ritual of any given society could thus miss the very different viewpoint of more discerning members of a culture, such as Kolean among the Santal. In the absence of that viewpoint, an outsider might easily come to the erroneous conclusion that Thakur Jiu was the name of a Santal sun god.

Take another case in point: Huascar, twelfth ruler of the Inca empire (Pachacuti was the ninth) actually set up a golden idol on an island in Lake Titicaca and called it *Viracocha*-Inti![29]

Pachacuti's mummy must have growled in its crypt!

The name of the Greek god *Zeus* is another example. Compare the name *Zeus* with the names *Theos* and *Deus* in the following column:

Zeus

Θeos (using the Greek consonant *theta* instead of "th")

Deus

One does not need a degree in linguistics to guess that all three names sprang from a single linguistic root. All three begin with consonants—Z, Θ and D—which require the tip of the tongue to be either between the teeth or immediately behind them. All three names feature what linguists call a "high front unrounded vowel—*e*" in the second slot. The third slot in all three names contains the "back rounded" vowels *o* or *u*. And all three names fill the fourth slot with the sibilant *s*. Finally, all three share similar meaning. Now for a theoretical reconstruction of the probable history of these three terms.

Originally, before Greek and Latin became differentiated as distinct languages, there was one mother term—*Deos*, perhaps—which was a personal name for the Almighty. Later, as various sects invented trendy lesser gods and gave them personal names, each sect claimed that its private god was actually *Deos*. As a result, by the time changes in pronunciation caused *Deos* to become *Deus* in one area, and Θ*eos* in another, all three terms had become generalized to mean "god" instead of "God."

To illustrate: Facial tissues first appeared under a brand name, Kleenex. By the time competing companies produced other brands of facial tissue, the word "Kleenex" was so indelibly associated with facial tissues that the public called the competing products "Kleenex" also. In other words, "Kleenex" had become "kleenex," just as *Deus* (God) became *deus* (god).

Philosophers such as Xenophanes, Plato and Aristotle in effect tried to reverse the trend toward generalization by returning to the original use of theos as a personal name. The result? Both the original specific and the later general meanings began to coexist.

Zeus, as a third variant of the original *Deos*, managed to avoid generalization, surviving as a specific personal name. In fact, Epimenides used *Zeus* as a personal name for the Almighty in another part of the very poem which Paul the apostle quoted in Titus 1:12! A different fate, however—and a far more serious one—befell the *Zeus* variant.

Greek theologians, tinkering through centuries with the Almighty's personal name *Zeus*, gradually introduced meanings that were inconsistent with the original concept. They decided, for example, to make Zeus the offspring of two other beings—Kronus and Rhea. Once theologians tricked worshipers into accepting their revision, the name *Zeus* no longer designated an uncreated Creator. In the absence of a sufficient number of "Koleans" to defend the original concept, *Zeus* died as a valid name for God. That once profound word went on to become so encrusted with barnacles of error that not even a Plato or an Aristotle could rescue it. They simply had to bypass it in favor of *Theos*. So also did Jewish translators and Christian apostles.

Likewise, almost as soon as Christianity was born, theological "meaning-changers" tried to insinuate trendy new meanings into Christian terms. The great theological councils of the church fathers can be understood as an attempt to keep meaningful Christian terms from suffering the same fate as once lofty words like *Zeus*.

One of the amazing characteristics of this benign, omnipotent "sky-god" of mankind's many folk religions is His propensity to identify Himself with the God of Christianity! For "sky-god," though regarded in most folk religions as remote and more or less unreachable, tends to draw near and speak to folk religionists whenever—unknown to themselves—they are about to meet emissaries of the Christian God!

And what does "sky-god" say at such times? Does he rant and rave jealously against the God of Christianity as an encroaching foreign deity? Does he urge his followers to fanatical rejection of the intruder's gospel? Far from it! In hundreds of instances attested to by literally millions of folk religionists worldwide, the Sky-God does exactly what *El Elyon* did through Melchizedek. He cheerfully acknowledges the approaching messengers of Yahweh as *His* messengers! He takes pains to make it very clear that He Himself is none other than the very God those particular foreigners proclaim!

One gains an unmistakable impression that the Sky-God wanted to communicate with people of various folk religions all the time, but for His own mysterious reasons maintained a policy of restraint until the arrival of Yahweh's testimony!

This is surely a powerful extrabiblical evidence for the authenticity of the Bible as revelation from the one true and universal God! It is also, as we shall see later, the prime reason on the human level for the phenomenal acceptance Christianity has found among people of many different folk religions worldwide. In addition, Scripture after Scripture has testified down through the centuries that our God has not left Himself without witness—even apart from the preaching of the gospel (see for example, Acts 14:16-17 and Romans 1:19-20; 2:14-15). That witness—though different in kind and quality from the biblical witness—is still a witness to Him!

How tragic then that Christians in general have been told almost nothing of this worldwide phenomenon of monotheistic presupposition underlying most of the world's folk religions! Many theologians—and even some missionaries whose ministries have been tremendously facilitated by the phenomenon—have nervously pushed this mind-expanding evidence into a closet.

Why? If you belong to a tradition which has been teaching Christians for centuries that the rest of the world sits in total darkness and knows zilch about God, it becomes a little embarrassing to have to say, "We have been wrong. In actual fact, more than 90 percent of this world's folk religions acknowledge at least the existence of God. Some even anticipate His redeeming concern for mankind."

The apostle John's statement that the world lies in spiritual wickedness (see 1 John 5:19) needs to be coupled with the apostle Paul's acknowledgment that God has not left Himself without witness. For that witness has penetrated the wickedness to some degree almost everywhere!

As the apostle John put it, "the light shines in the darkness, but the darkness has not overpowered it" (John 1:5). John further specified that the "light" he describes is "the true light that gives light to *every* man" (1:9, emphasis added).

But why would missionaries who have experienced the sky-god phenomenon firsthand downplay the evidence? Perhaps they thought that some people back home might say, "See! They already had their own belief in God! You didn't have to go to them after all!" Avoiding the objection was easier than countering it—though it is easy enough to counter! So they simply communicated other important information to their supporters.

Other missionaries, trained under theologians who downplayed the phenomenon, were thereby mentally conditioned to ignore the evidence before they even encountered it! Or perhaps they were amazed by the evidence but felt reluctant to mention it lest their own teachers should question their orthodoxy.

Two or three prominent theologians—when they first began hearing second- or third-hand reports of nearly universal acknowledgment of a Supreme God within folk religions around the world—jumped to an ill-founded conclusion: The uniqueness of the Bible as God's sole inspired revelation of Himself to mankind, they thought, was being threatened. Indeed, some evolutionists, realizing that it would not go well for their cause if theologians began publicizing the sky-god phenomenon, cleverly spooked them into rejecting the phenomenon by insinuating that it proved that the Bible was not unique. The theologians responded unwisely by rejecting the sky-god phenomenon as being of no consequence. They in turn persuaded generations of their students to adopt the same defensive posture. Ever since, some theologians have made it part of their career to discredit Bible-paralleling beliefs in folk religions as "distortions" or "satanic counterfeits."

It is true, of course, that falsehoods, distortions and spiritual coun-terfeits do exist in the world. It is also possible for bearers of the gospel to get sidetracked by them, just as it is possible for a bee buzzing among blossoms to bumble into a Venus flytrap by mistake. But bees do not call a halt to nectar gathering because of danger from Venus flytraps. Or spi-derwebs. Or praying mantises (which are really preying mantises!).

Following are two examples of "Venus flytraps" posing as "blos-soms" in our "field," as Jesus repeatedly called this world. Missionaries do well to avoid such things and theologians justly warn us against them.

First, Hindus anticipate what they call "the tenth incarnation of Vishnu." A young missionary in India, desperate to gain the attention of Hindus, decided to proclaim Jesus Christ as simply that—the tenth incarnation of Vishnu! Surely he must have had his tongue in both cheeks at the same time when he said it. Conservative theologians justly wave their arms like umpires and cry "foul!" against such a compromising approach to cross-cultural communication.

They should not, however, with their next breath argue from one such instance that the viewpoint of other cultures is basically irrelevant when one approaches those cultures with the gospel. That sort of deduc-tion is an example of throwing the baby out with the bathwater.

The fact remains that Hindu belief in the possibility of deity becom-ing incarnate among men makes us more understandable when we talk to Hindus about "the Word who became flesh, and dwelt among us"—not on successive occasions but once and for all time!

Second, some Buddhists, likewise, anticipate a fifth manifestation of the Buddha as Phra-Ariya-Metrai—*the "lord of mercy."* It would be both wrong and futile to reduce the once-incarnated Son of God to a mere "fifth manifestation" of anyone. Yet Buddhist acknowledgment that mankind needs mercy administered by a power beyond himself remains a poten-tial point of contact.

Testimony among folk religions concerning the existence of the Supreme God tends, however, to constitute a category very different from the above. Following are two examples. One is from Harold Fuller's *Run While the Sun Is Hot*, with details added from Albert Brant's still unpublished *In the Footsteps of the Flock*. The other is from a personal interview with Dr. Eugene Rosenau, a virtual citizen of Central African Republic.

ETHIOPIA'S GEDEO PEOPLE

Deep in the hill country of south-central Ethiopia live several million coffee-growing people who, though divided into quite different tribes, share common belief in a benevolent being called *Magano*—omnipotent Creator of all that is. One of these tribes is called variously the *Darassa* or—more accurately—the Gedeo people. Few of the Gedeo tribe's half-million members actually prayed to *Magano*. In fact, a casual observer would have found the people far more concerned to appease an evil being they called *Sheit'an*. One day Albert Brant asked a group of Gedeo, "How is it that you regard Magano with profound awe, yet sacrifice to *Sheit'an*?" He received the following reply: "We sacrifice to *Sheit'an*, not because we love him, but because we simply do not enjoy close enough ties with *Magano* to allow us to be done with *Sheit'an*!"

At least one Gedeo man, however, did pursue a personal response from *Magano*. His name—Warrasa Wange. His status—related to the Gedeo tribe's "royal family." His domicile—a town called Dilla, located on an extreme edge of Gedeo tribal land. His method of approach to *Magano*—a simple prayer asking *Magano* to reveal Himself to the Gedeo people!

Warrasa Wange got speedy response. Startling visions took his brain by storm. He saw two white-skinned strangers. ("Caucasophobes"—people who dislike or fear "white men," commonly called Caucasians—will object, but what can I do? History must not have anticipated the modern trend toward caucasophobia!)

Warrasa saw the two whites erect flimsy shelters for themselves under the shade of a large sycamore tree near Dilla, Warrasa's hometown. Later they built more permanent shiny-roofed structures. Eventually these structures dotted an entire hillside! Never had the dreamer seen anything even faintly resembling either the flimsy temporary structures or the shiny-roofed permanent ones. All dwellings in Gedeo land were grass-roofed.

Then Warrasa heard a voice. "These men," it said, "will bring you a message from *Magano*, the God you seek. Wait for them."

In a final scene of his vision, Warrasa saw himself remove the center pole from his own house. In Gedeo symbolism, the center pole of a man's house stands for his very life. He then carried that center pole out of the town and set it in the ground next to one of the shiny-roofed dwellings of the strange men.

Warrasa understood the implication—his life must later stand in identification with those strange men, their message, and with *Magano* who would send them.

Warrasa waited. Eight years passed. During those eight years several other soothsayers among the Gedeo people prophesied that strangers would soon arrive with a message from *Magano*.

Then, one very hot day in December 1948, blue-eyed Canadian Albert Brant and his colleague Glen Cain lurched over the horizon in a battered old International truck. Their mission—to begin missionary work for the glory of God among the Gedeo people. They had hoped to gain permission from Ethiopian officials to locate their new mission at the very center of the Gedeo region, but Ethiopians friendly to the mission advised that such a request would meet certain refusal due to the current political climate.

"Ask only to go as far as this town called Dilla," the advisors said with a wink. "It is quite distant from the center of the tribe. Those opposed to your mission will think you couldn't possibly influence the entire tribe from such a peripheral town!"

"There it is," Brant said to Cain. "It's only the very edge of the Gedeo population, but it will have to do."

With a sigh, he turned the old International toward Dilla. Glen Cain wiped sweat from his brow. "This is a hot one, Albert," he said. "I hope we can find a shady spot for our tents!"

"Look at that old sycamore tree!" Albert responded. "Just what the doctor ordered!"

Brant revved the International up a rise toward the sycamore. In the distance, Warrasa Wange heard the sound. He turned just in time to see

Brant's old truck pull to a stop under the sycamore's spreading branches. Slowly Warrasa headed toward the truck, wondering . . .

Three decades later Warrasa (now a radiant believer in Jesus Christ,
Son of *Magano*), together with Albert Brant and others, counted more
than 200 churches among the Gedeo people—churches averaging more
than 200 members each! With the help of Warrasa and other inhabitants
of Dilla, almost the entire Gedeo tribe has been influenced by the gospel—in spite of Dilla's peripheral location!

Central African Republic's Mbaka People

What happened among the Gedeo is by no means an isolated incident.
Incredible as it seems, literally thousands of Christian missionaries
down through history have been startled by the exuberant welcome,
even from some of Earth's remotest peoples! Folk who could not have
read a newspaper even if one were dropped on their doorstep anticipated the coming of message-bearers for the true God almost as knowl-
edgeably as if they had just read about them in the morning news!
Usually, however, the "sky-god"—as anthropologists commonly designate Him—would not reveal just what kind of good news His message-
bearers would bring. He preferred only to say they were coming. That is
why the story of *Koro* is such an amazing exception!

Koro? The Creator as designated in several Bantu languages of Africa.
And one Bantu tribe—the Mbaka—came closer perhaps than any other
people on Earth to anticipating not merely the arrival of a message from
Koro but even part of its actual content!

The Mbaka live near the town of Sibyut in the Central African
Republic. Missionary Eugene Rosenau, Ph.D., used to listen spellbound
whenever Mbaka tribesmen—especially those from Yablangba village—
explained why they responded to the gospel with such immediacy when
Eugene's father Ferdinand Rosenau and his Baptist colleagues first
preached among the Mbaka in the early 1920s.

One day Eugene, deeply moved, exclaimed: "Your Mbaka ancestors
were closer to the truth than my Germanic forefathers in northern

Europe!" Following are some comments from Mbaka tribesmen relayed to me from Mbakaland by Eugene Rosenau himself.

"*Koro*, the Creator, sent word to our forefathers long ages ago that He has already sent His Son into the world to accomplish something wonderful for all mankind. Later, however, our forefathers turned away from the truth about *Koro*'s Son. In time they even forgot what it was that He accomplished for mankind. Since the time of 'the forgetting,' successive generations of our people have longed to discover the truth about *Koro*'s Son. But all we could learn was that messengers would eventually come to restore that forgotten knowledge to us. Somehow we knew also that the messengers would probably be white-skinned. . . ."

("Caucasophobes," relax! This time the whiteness was only a probability!)

" . . . In any case, we resolved that whenever *Koro*'s messengers arrived we would all welcome them and believe their message!"

Ferdinand Rosenau discovered, moreover, that men of a certain large village called Yablangba were considered "keepers of the lore of *Koro*"—a sort of Levitical clan within the tribe. How, then, did they respond to the gospel?

Mbaka people in Yablangba, Eugene says, responded so thoroughly to the gospel that by the 1950s someone made a startling discovery— 75 to 80 percent of all African pastors trained by Eugene and his colleagues were from that one very large village—Yablangba! The percentage later altered as other responsive peoples of Central African Republic began contributing their share of leaders, most of whom were instructed, of course, by the original Yablangba pastors.

Even tribal "rites of passage" among the Mbaka, Eugene says, show Judeo-Christian parallels. First, the elders offered a blood sacrifice for the initiate. Then they baptized the initiate by immersion in a river. For several days following his baptism, the initiate must behave like a newborn child! In keeping with the imagery, he is not permitted to talk.

Whenever a Mbaka man tripped over a stone, he would first turn and gratefully anoint the offending object. Then he would say to it, "Tell me, stone, was *Koro* using you to keep me from danger or from evil?"

Eugene sees an amazing parallel between that custom and the biblical metaphor of Jesus Christ as a "stone of stumbling" and a "rock of offence." He is such, however, only to men who do not recognize that God is seeking to keep them from danger and from evil through Him! The Mbaka, for their part, are determined to acknowledge *Koro*'s blessing even when it comes disguised as a troublesome stone that hurts one's foot!

Eugene recalls a time years ago when younger missionaries, delighted by similar nuggets from Mbaka lore, said they would like "more time to study the culture." An older missionary objected, "One does not study hell. One preaches heaven!"

Granted, "hell" is present always in every human society. Noble "savages" are just as rare as noble civilizados. The same man who "anoints the rock" one day may commit murder the next. Granted also, we must never allow our fascination with any human situation to so absorb us that we fail to "preach heaven."

Nevertheless, it seems clear that "hell" didn't quite have everything its own way in the development of Mbaka culture. Some influence of "heaven" came through. And anyone who truly wanted to preach heaven to the Mbaka was not amiss if he first studied the influence heaven had already exerted within their world!

Just as we ourselves accept a stranger readily if he has first been recommended by someone we know and trust, so also the Mbaka received the gospel joyfully because it was first recommended to them by something they knew and trusted—their own lore regarding *Koro*!

For these reasons I propose that these particular facets of Mbaka lore be described as "redemptive." (*Note*: "redemptive," not "redeeming"! "Redeeming" would mean that Mbaka people could find relationship with God through their own lore, apart from the gospel. "Redemptive" in this context means "contributing to the redemption of a people, but not culminating it.")

"Redemptive lore" contributes to the redemption of a people solely by facilitating their understanding of what redemption means.

Their own redemptive lore caused Mbaka people to see the gospel as something to be treasured, not as something imposed arbitrarily by a foreigner. That same gospel fitted not only *Koro*'s requirements as a righteous God, but also their own needs as guilty men and women. The fact that the gospel could do this in a way that fulfilled rather than destroyed this "redemptive" heart of Mbaka lore makes the gospel more unique, not less! That uniqueness increases a thousand fold when we discover that the same gospel also fulfills the redemptive components of a thousand other cultures as well!

No other message on Earth has an inside track already laid for it in the belief systems of thousands of very different human societies!

How sad that some theologians thought the gospel's uniqueness was being threatened by such lore when actually it was enhanced! How sad also that they have taught us to condemn such lore as "counterfeit" or as "distortion." This kind of teaching has caused some Christians—including some missionaries—to be very defensive if not actually offensive toward non-Christian people. It has caused them to view Christian-like parallels in other cultures as barriers to the gospel, rather than as thresholds with "welcome!" written across them!

Another question—what if converts among a given people, after receiving the gospel with understanding facilitated by their own lore, later become disenchanted with the gospel? What if they even turn back to their own lore and make it an end in itself? What if they build a cult around it in competition with the church of Jesus Christ? Should we then say, "Aha! This proves that their lore was of the devil all along!"

Not so! If a wife ruins her husband's razor by using it to cut linoleum, does that mean he should not have kept a razor in the first place? Subsequent misuse does not invalidate the razor's intended purpose. Before discrediting the lore or blaming the people for their action we should first ask ourselves questions such as the following.

In our appropriation of the lore, did we leave too many questions unanswered? Or have second- or third-generation missionaries perhaps failed to appreciate the cross-cultural methodology of the hardy pioneers who first achieved rapport with people in their area? Occasionally as I visit mission fields I find that missionaries following through on work started by others have never even thought to inquire what sort of communication their predecessors found effective. If these successors take too much for granted, they may unnecessarily offend young converts, driving them away from Christian churches. Then if those converts seek to fill the void in their lives by affirming ancient lore which they know instinctively is somehow related to the gospel, the lore may unjustly be dubbed as a "tool Satan uses to beguile young converts."

Still another question—is it not humiliating to peoples like the Gedeo or the Mbaka to know about *Magano/Koro* and yet have to wait centuries until foreigners in some other part of the world decide that "perhaps it is time we went and told them how they can know Him personally"?

The answer is, first of all, yes! People like the Gedeo or the Mbaka have often put missionaries on the spot, asking: "Did your great-grandfather know the way to God? He did? Then why didn't he come and tell my great-grandfather?"

But a more complete answer requires also the following comment: Think of the most conceited, most arrogant people you know (not counting yourself). Now ask: What common denominator lurks behind that conceit and that arrogance? Invariably that common denominator is simply a delusion of independence—a narrow-minded confidence in one's ability to forge one's destiny.

And if among the conceited people, you find one who thinks he has also made himself pleasing even to God—he is sure to be the most conceited of them all! Little wonder then that God's answer to human conceit is to declare all of us *dependent*! Dependent not upon our own "good works" but upon His Son's good work on Calvary! This leaves us all with not a single basis for boasting! But God seems to have gone even further . . .

In addition to rendering us dependent upon His Son for salvation, He has also reduced us to dependence upon our fellowman for news about that salvation! Jesus Himself published no book. In fact, He left us not a single letter in His own handwriting! Nor has He in this age assigned angels to preach the gospel, either instead of or along with men!

If He added angels to His communications task force, you can guess what would happen—churches founded through the ministry of angels would proclaim their superiority over churches founded by the ministry of mere men (or vice versa)!

In God's economy, however, things tend to work in ways that provide no fertilizer for human pride! "God opposes the proud, but gives grace to the humble" (1 Pet. 5:5). So if it will prompt humility in a Jew to have a Samaritan teach him a spiritual lesson, God will gladly arrange an appropriate teaching situation! (See Luke 10:25-37; 17:11-17.) Likewise, God sometimes humbles proud Europeans by speaking His truth to them through brown or black brothers from Asia or Africa. Conversely, it may be best for the soul of a resentful liberationist if he finds the way of true liberation through a member of the hated dominant race!

With these principles in mind, I choose not to question God's way of using unlikely messengers to reach various peoples. I fully expect He will continue to employ messengers who cause eyebrows in at least one quarter to rise!

Now for another example or two of prepared peoples.

THE CHINESE AND THE KOREANS

The Chinese call him *Shang Ti*—the Lord of Heaven.

Some scholars speculate that *Shang Ti* may even be related linguistically to the Hebrew term *Shaddai*, as in *El Shaddai*, the Almighty.

In Korea he is known as *Hananim*—The Great One.

Belief in *Shang Ti/Hananim* predates Confucianism, Taoism and Buddhism by an unknown number of centuries. In fact, according to the *Encyclopedia of Religion and Ethics*, the first reference in Chinese history to any kind of religious belief specifies Shang Ti alone as the object of that belief.[30] The antiquity of that reference—an estimated 2,600 years before Christ! That is more than 2,000 years before Confucianism or any other structured religion arose in China!

Worshipers throughout both China and Korea seem to have understood from the beginning that *Shang Ti/Hananim* must never be represented by idols. Chinese people, for their part, appear to have paid homage to *Shang Ti* quite freely until the dawn of the Zhou Dynasty (1066–770 B.C.). By that time, Chinese religious leaders—zealous to emphasize *Shang Ti*'s majesty and holiness—gradually lost sight of His love and mercy toward men. Soon they worked themselves into a corner so constricted that only the emperor was deemed "good enough" to worship *Shang Ti*—and that only once a year!

Common people, from that time forward, were forbidden to pay homage to their Creator directly. Father Emperor would take care of everything, they were told.

Tragic parallels bond this ancient Chinese policy with Inca Pachacuti's decision to limit to upper classes only the privilege of worshiping *Viracocha*. Pachacuti's decision not only left the masses without *Viracocha*, it also left *Viracocha* without followers among the Incas once conquistadores obliterated the upper class of Incadom. Likewise, Chinese imperial policy not only left the masses without *Shang Ti*, it also left *Shang Ti* virtually without adherents among the Chinese because of what followed.

Cutting the masses off from their customary obeisance to *Shang Ti* created a spiritual vacuum in China. That vacuum could not exist for long without something rushing in to fill it. Surely it must be significant that within a mere three centuries of the end of the Zhou Dynasty, three entirely new religions materialized out of nowhere and rushed in to try to fill that vacuum.

The first, Confucianism, began by teaching the masses to limit religious devotion to ancestor worship while giving priority to the development of a better society here on Earth! Never mind about *Shang Ti*, Confucius advised. He is far too high and unapproachable for common people. Just leave Him to the emperor who alone can mediate on your behalf! In other words, Confucianism simply tried to build a humanistic structure around the status quo! Ancestor worship was a sop Confucianism used to tranquilize man's religious instinct, not satisfy it!

Favored by the ruling class for obvious reasons, Confucianism began gaining ground. Confucius's teachings could not, however, satisfy the religious instinct of a large majority of Chinese. The result: Taoism arose as a would-be popular alternative to Confucianism.

Taoism's solution for the hunger aching in Chinese hearts was a mixture of magic, philosophy and mystical formulae. Taoists ridiculed

Confucius's quest for an ideal human society. Universal order, Taoists declared, staunchly favors the status quo and would stubbornly resist all attempts to improve it!

Taoism also began gaining ground, but the hunger continued. Then it came—over the Himalayas from India. A new religion called Buddhism. It seems incredible that Buddhism could have found a welcome in China, for Buddhism emphasized celibacy. Nothing could be more abominable to the Chinese with their overwhelming idealization of marriage and procreation! Nevertheless, Buddhism rapidly gained widespread popular support and eventually overshadowed both Confucianism and Taoism as the predominant religion of China.[31]

Why did Buddhism succeed?

First, Buddhist teachers avoided confrontation with contrary indigenous patterns. They constantly changed or adapted their doctrines to make them acceptable to Chinese. Buddhism just melted into Chinese society like hot butter into fresh bread. For the stubborn majority who scorned celibacy, Buddhist priests obligingly devised other ways married Chinese could earn Brownie points in their quest for Nirvana.

But the main reason by far for Buddhism's acceptance by China's millions was a very straightforward one—Buddhism demonstrated willingness to provide gods which the Chinese could worship!

Not that Gautama, founder of Buddhism, intended his followers to teach idolatry. He even warned them, in fact, not to start a new religion! Buddhism began only as a reaction to excesses within Hinduism. Originally Buddhism was just as man-centered as Confucianism, if not more so!

Gautama's followers, however, soon came to the pragmatic conclusion that worship-starved masses in China wanted deities they could bow down to, not just man-centered ideals they could look up to! Buddhist priests saw an opportunity to upstage not only humanistic Confucianism but also mystical Taoism with its philosophy, magic and ritual. But did they advocate a return to the worship of Shang Ti? To do so would have been to infringe upon a domain the emperor considered his own. There was one very enticing alternative.

They encouraged the Chinese to worship Gautama himself as *Buddha*—the enlightened one! Gautama's dust must have turned to lye and eaten its way through the floor of his tomb! Since the Chinese had trouble forming a mental picture of an Indian Gautama, Buddhist priests fashioned appropriately slant-eyed statues of him. Just as an aid to worship, mind you! In time, someone advocated burning incense in front of the commemorative statues. Again, be assured, it was simply an aid to worship. Nothing to fret about. Before long everyone knew the statues had become idols for worship, but by then no one cared.

Buddhism provided gods, yes, but not *the* God. *Shang Ti*, the God to whom many of China's founding fathers prayed, had no part in Buddhism, nor did He desire any. *Shang Ti*, whose providence—according to China's own historians—had made her a great nation, was no longer listed as a God to whom common people might pray.

Just as Inti worship—the Sodom factor among the Incas—almost totally obscured the memory of *Viracocha*, so also Buddhism became the Sodom factor which almost totally distracted the majority of Chinese and—some time later—the majority of Koreans, from *Shang Ti/Hananim*.

Almost.

In spite of the concerted distraction of three competing religions, the haunting memory of *Shang Ti* lingered. Even as long as two-and-a-half millennia after the emergence of Confucianism, Taoism and Buddhism, Chinese and Koreans still spoke occasionally of *Shang Ti/Hananim* with curiosity and a certain reverence. Occasionally, too, Chinese children would say, "Pappa, tell us about *Shang Ti*." Korean children would exclaim, "Pappa, tell us about *Hananim*." Invariably, both Chinese and Korean fathers would shake their heads and say, "We know so little. He is far away."

As *Viracocha*, *Shang Ti* was to have his Pachacuti. But as *Shang Ti* or as *Hananim*, where would He find advocates to plead for the return of unfaithful peoples?

This time, emissaries bearing *Shang Ti/Hananim*'s special revelation—the Judeo-Christian testimony—arrived. Their testimony, however, was often intermittent. Neither did these messengers to Chinese and later to Korean peoples always identify their testimony with the residual monotheistic witness already acknowledged by Chinese and Koreans as valid.

Instead of calling their listeners to kneel in repentance before *Shang Ti/Hananim*—the God reverenced by founding fathers of both nations before the dawn of written history—the messengers sometimes deliberately imposed a completely foreign name for the Almighty. At times they took pains to emphasize that this "foreign" God was like no god which Chinese or Koreans had ever heard of before. Those who took this position completely misunderstood the real situation. They also missed the real point of their own ministries. It was as if Abraham had refused to acknowledge *El Elyon*.

First to arrive: Nestorians, in the eighth century A.D. Later, Kublai Khan, fascinated by what he had learned of the gospel from Marco Polo, sent messengers to the pope requesting missionaries to come and teach the good news about Jesus Christ to all the peoples of his empire. His empire, at that time, included China. The pope belatedly sent four priests on their way to the Khan's domain. Some of them died on the way and others turned back out of fear.

Convinced that monotheism was superior to idolatry, Kublai Khan turned to Islam instead. As a result, many Mongolian peoples eventually became Muslims.

Still later, Roman Catholic orders reached China and Korea with mixed results. Roman Catholics adopted phrases like *Tien Ju*, Master of Heaven, or *Tien Laoye* to designate God in the Chinese language. Later in Korea they ignored for many decades the native term *Hananim* and imposed in its place these same Chinese terms.

Protestant missionaries, when finally they reached China, disagreed vehemently among themselves as to whether they should use *Shang Ti*, some other Chinese word or phrase, or a foreign term for the Almighty. One party argued that it was better to use "a new name for a new thing." Those who employed *Shang Ti* usually did not exploit the full potential of the name by evoking its very ancient association with China's origins. Lack of unanimity on this vital question was probably the main reason why Protestants made proportionately less impact upon China than they did upon Korea.

For when Protestant missionaries entered Korea in 1884, they found themselves virtually unanimous! Records indicate that Protestants genuinely believed, after investigating Korean understanding of the supernatural world, that Yahweh could have only one name in Korea—*Hananim*! Some, perhaps, chose *Hananim* out of sheer orneriness. They saw that using it would enable them to upstage Roman Catholic missionaries who preceded Protestants in some parts of Korea, but were imposing a foreign name for God.

In any case, as early as 1890 one Protestant pioneer wrote: "The name Hannonim is so distinctive and so universally used that there will be no fear, in future translations and preachings, of the unseemly squabbles which occurred long ago among Chinese missionaries on this subject— even though the Romanists have introduced the name which they employ in China."[32]

Whether based upon conviction or contrariness, the choice of *Hananim* could not have been more providential for Protestant missions in Korea! Preaching like houses afire in cities, towns, villages or in the countryside, Protestant missionaries began by affirming Korean belief in *Hananim*. Building upon this residual witness, Protestants masterfully disarmed the Korean people's natural antipathy toward bowing before some foreign deity. Speaking directly to a public already wistfully curious about *Hananim*, Protestants echoed the apostle Paul's proclamation at Lystra: "In the past, [*Theos*] let all peoples [including Koreans] go their own way [choosing Shamanism, Confucianism or Buddhism in preference to Him]; yet he did not leave himself without witness" (see Acts 14:16-17).

Following through, Protestants explained that *Hananim* had laid the groundwork for a future reconciliation with repentant peoples by revealing Himself in a new way to one people—the Jews. He chose the Jews, not because they were greater in number or better in quality than other peoples, but simply because He needed a specific lens to focus a new revelation of Himself upon the screen of human history.

He also gave that revelation in actual written form through specific men—Moses, the prophets and the apostles. Most important of all, He incarnated His own Son among the Jews. Jesus the Messiah—the Eternal Logos, the only Righteous Man—died for the sins of all peoples and then rose from the dead, proving to all men that Hananim accepted His atonement. Then He commissioned messengers bearing good news of redemption to all peoples, calling all peoples to repentance and faith in the name of Jesus, Son of *Hananim*.

Koreans by the thousands listened to the Protestants with awe. Here were men and women who knew ever so much more about the true God than even their own king who paid homage to him yearly on a sacred island in the river near Pyongyang, capital of Korea.[33] Here were people who prayed freely to *Hananim* in the name of this Jesus, and received answers to those prayers.

Koreans were impressed. One of their own *Tan'gun* traditions affirmed that *Hananim* had a Son who desired to live among men.[34] Catholic missionaries, still designating God with Chinese phrases like *Tien Ju* or *Tien Laoye*, seemed to Koreans to imply that Chinese culture was superior to Korean ways. Koreans in those days had a hard enough time as it was trying not to feel inferior to their highly literate and scientifically more sophisticated Chinese neighbors. Koreans in increasing numbers began giving ear to Protestant missionaries. Soon, momentous response to the gospel of Jesus Christ began to shake much of Korea! Today, a little over a century after the first Protestants arrived, approximately 9.5 million Koreans belong to Protestant churches.[35]

Protestants also did at least one other thing right in Korea. They insisted that Korean churches become self-governing, self-supporting and self-propagating almost from birth! A baby, if proper care is taken, can afford to have its umbilical cord cut minutes after birth. A baby may even, if proper care is taken, learn to swim in the first few weeks of its life! So also infant churches, with adequate teaching and example, can stand on their own in remarkably short periods of time.

Early missionaries in Korea "took the proper care" and some very strong churches resulted. Seoul, Korea, for example, is home to the largest Protestant church in the world—the Yoido Full Gospel Church, which reached a membership of 780,000 in 2003! The membership of that one congregation exceeds the entire population of many cities.[36]

David Yonggi Cho, the pastor, has organized the Yoido Full Gospel Church into nearly 25,000 cell groups.[37] Each cell has its own trained leadership. If any unfriendly power should try to repress South Korean

Christianity, the Yoido Full Gospel Church is prepared to scatter its thousands of cell groups like spores in the wind. In that event, the massive building where the church now meets would become an empty husk, but witness would continue.

Another of the largest Protestant congregations in the world that is located in South Korea is Young Nak Presbyterian, which is currently climbing past the 60,000-member mark. According to Dr. Sam Moffat, Jr., Young Nak is also a prolific mother church. Hundreds of daughter churches in Seoul and surrounding suburbs trace their origin to the witness of Young Nak.[38]

What of Roman Catholic churches in Korea? According to Dr. Sam Moffat, Jr., Roman Catholic priests in Korea, seeing Protestant churches flourish while their own parishes by comparison were growing slowly, held a conference to ask themselves "What are we doing wrong?" Interestingly, they decided they had made a mistake when they rejected the name *Hananim* in favor of non-Korean names for the Almighty. They decided to use the name *Hananim* from that time forward.

They called in more priests and launched a fresh preaching campaign throughout Korea. Their purpose: to identify themselves strongly, if belatedly, with Hananim! From that time forward, Catholicism began to experience a faster rate of growth. Roman Catholic churches in South Korea now total approximately 3.5 million members, bringing Christendom's total constituency in South Korea—after a mere 120 years of uninterrupted growth—to approximately 27.3 percent of the entire population.[39] It is not clear whether Catholicism will ever be able to overtake the numerical lead Protestants have gained, mainly by choosing a Korean name for God and then placing the leadership of churches in Korean hands as early as possible!

As the Lord tarries, South Korea may well become the first nation on Earth to see more than 50 percent of its entire population enrolled as members of Protestant churches. Nor do our Korean brethren rely upon the arm of flesh! Predawn prayer meetings in Korean churches characteristically overflow with thousands of earnest supplicants. Their main prayer request—the conversion of their brothers and sisters in North Korea from communism to Christ!

And whenever winds blow from south to north along the demilita-
rized zone, Korean Christians range along hilltops and release balloons
loaded with Bibles toward their brothers and sisters beyond the zone.

Hananim must have His witness there as well![40]

CHAPTER 2

Peoples of the Lost Book

THE KAREN OF BURMA

Near Rangoon, Burma, in the year 1795, an encounter took place in the following manner:

"If the inhabitants of that village are not Burmese," asked a sun-helmeted English diplomat, "what do they call themselves?"

"Karen," replied the diplomat's Burmese guide.

"Carian," mispronounced the Englishman. The guide left the mistake uncorrected. A Scotsman could have duplicated the Asiatic flipping the tongue on an *r* but the guide had long ago given up trying to persuade Englishmen that the difference was worth mastering.

"Very well," said the Britisher. "Let's see what these 'Carianers' look like."

The "Carianers," it turned out, were even more interested to discover what the Englishman looked like! This first encounter with a European's white face electrified people in that village. Drawn like moths to a lamp, they converged upon the diplomat, who recoiled slightly as wiry brown hands reached out to touch his arms and cheeks.

The Burmese guide, meanwhile, spoke disparagingly of the Karen: "Be careful! They're just wild hill people given to stealing and fighting," he scoffed.

It was not entirely true. The Karen were in fact the most progressive of Burma's many tribal peoples. Burmese, however, had abused and exploited the Karen for centuries, making such descriptions self-fulfilling.

Nor could Burmese Buddhists forgive the Karen minority for stubbornly adhering to their own folk religion in the face of unremitting attempts by the Burmese to make Buddhists of them!

The Englishman, in any case, was no longer listening to his guide. Cheerful Karen voices now charmed his ears. Every man, woman and child around him glowed with radiant welcome. How refreshingly different, he thought, from the usual Burmese crowd's aloofness toward foreigners.

A Karen man who could speak Burmese explained something to the guide.

"This is most interesting," the guide said. "These tribesmen think you may be a certain 'white brother' whom they as a people have been expecting from time immemorial!"

"How curious," replied the diplomat. "Ask them what this 'white brother' is supposed to do when he arrives."

"He's supposed to bring them a book," the guide said. "A book just like one their forefathers lost long ago. They are asking—with bated breath— "hasn't he brought it?'"

"Ho! Ho!" the Englishman guffawed. "And who, pray tell, is the author whose book has power to charm illiterate folk like these?"

"They say the author is *Y'wa*—the Supreme God. They say also . . ." at this point the Burman's face began to darken with unease, ". . . that the white brother, having given them the lost book, will thereby set them free from all who oppress them."

The Burman began to fidget. The nerve of these Karen! This English diplomat was part of a team sent to arbitrate a dispute between Britain and Burma—a dispute which Burma feared might give Britain pretext to add Burma to its empire. And now these wily Karen were practically inviting the British to do just that! Who would have guessed, he fumed, that simple tribesmen could be capable of such subtlety?

Sensing the guide's displeasure, the Englishman also began to squirm. One word from the guide and Burmese authorities might descend with swords and spears against these humble villagers.

"Tell them they're mistaken," he ordered, hoping to set the Burman at ease. "I have no acquaintance with this god called *Y'wa*. Nor do I have the slightest idea who their 'white brother' could be."

Followed by the guide, the diplomat strode out of the village. Hundreds of Karen, palled with disappointment, watched him leave. They intended no political ploy. They had simply repeated in all sincerity a tradition which had haunted them as a people since antiquity.

"Could our forefathers have been mistaken?" asked a young Karen.

"Don't worry," responded an elder, managing a hopeful smile. "One day he will come. Other prophecies may fail, but not this one!"

Returning to the newly established British embassy in Rangoon, the diplomat reported his strange experience in the Karen village to his superior, Lieutenant Colonel Michael Symes. Symes in turn mentioned it in a manuscript entitled *An Account of an Embassy to the Kingdom of Ava in the Year 1795*, published 32 years later in Edinburgh, Scotland.

For the next 175 years, occasional browsers in Symes' report paid scant attention, if any, to this curious reference on Karen tradition. Its anecdotal nature effectively screened its historical significance. Nineteenth century Britishers, moreover, were not generally interested in approaching Asians as a "white brother." White master was a role more to their liking. Indeed, beginning in 1824, Britain launched a series of attacks against Burma and eventually became, for about one century, rulers of that exotic land.

Even before the first British invasion, however, history recorded a second foreigner's encounter with the Karen people's lost book tradition.

In the year 1816 a Muslim traveler happened to enter a remote Karen village about 250 miles south of Rangoon. The Karen scrutinized him carefully as they had scrutinized all foreigners who ever came their way—especially light-skinned ones—looking for their "white brother." Well, the Muslim was not very light-skinned, but he did have in his possession a book. And he said the book contained writings about the true God.

Seeing their intense fascination with the book, the Muslim offered it as a gift to an elderly Karen sage. Later the people said he told them to worship it, but it seems unlikely that a Muslim would give that kind of advice. Perhaps he simply urged them to take good care of it until one day, hopefully, a teacher would come who could interpret it for them.

The Muslim continued his journey, and never returned.

The sage who received the little book wrapped it in muslin and placed it in a special basket. Gradually the people developed rituals for venerating the sacred volume. The sage adorned himself with ornate garments befitting his role as keeper of the book. He carried a special cudgel as a symbol of his spiritual authority. And, most poignant of all, he and his people kept constant vigil for the teacher who would one day come to their village and open the contents of the sacred book to their understanding.[1]

But that is not all. In perhaps a thousand or more Karen villages of Burma, men called *Bukhos*, a special kind of teacher representing not demons but *Y'wa*, the true God—yes, the Karen actually esteemed them as prophets of the true God—kept reminding the Karen that the ways of *Y'wa* and the ways of *nats* (evil spirits) were not the same. One day, these Bukhos affirmed, the Karen people must return fully to the ways of *Y'wa*.

Karen prophets actually taught their people hymns passed down from generation to generation by verbal communication alone. Like Pachacuti's hymns to *Viracocha*, Karen hymns to *Y'wa* reveal how astonishingly clear the concept of the one true God can be in a folk religion! By means of these hymns, awe and reverence for *Y'wa*, the true God, were kept alive in the hearts of Karen people so that they would not lapse into Buddhism with its idolatry. One such hymn extolled the eternity of *Y'wa*'s being:

Y'wa is eternal, his life is long.
One aeon—he dies not!
Two aeons—he dies not!
He is perfect in meritorious attributes.
Aeons follow aeons—he dies not![2]

Another hymn extolled *Y'wa* as Creator:

Who created the world in the beginning?
Y'wa created the world in the beginning!
Y'wa appointed everything.
Y'wa is unsearchable![3]

Still another hymn conveyed deep appreciation for *Y'wa*'s omnipotence and omniscience, combined with acknowledgment of a lack of relationship with Him:

The omnipotent is Y'wa; him have we not believed.
Y'wa created men anciently;
He has a perfect knowledge of all things!
Y'wa created men at the beginning;
He knows all things to the present time!
O my children and grandchildren!
The earth is the treading place of the feet of Y'wa.
And heaven is the place where he sits.
He sees all things, and we are manifest to him.[4]

The Karen story of man's falling away from God contains stunning parallels to Genesis chapter 1:

Y'wa formed the world originally.
He appointed food and drink.
He appointed the "fruit of trial."
He gave detailed orders.
Mu-kaw-lee [Satan] deceived two persons.

He caused them to eat the fruit of the tree of trial.
They obeyed not; they believed not Y'wa . . .
When they ate the fruit of trial,
They became subject to sickness, aging, and death. . . .[5]

An author named Alonzo Bunker, who lived among the Karen for 30 years during the late nineteenth century, describes a typical late-evening teaching session in the jungle led by Karen Bukhos near Toungoo, Burma:

It is quite impossible to describe the solemn and reverential manner in which these white-haired elders recited the attributes of Y'wa, and with what awed attention the children listened . . . they were drawn as a magnet to this council of elders. For a while there was silence, save the crackling of bamboo and brush in the fire. And then the old prophet of the village . . . arose and extended his hands, as if in benediction, and said:

"O children and grandchildren, formerly Y'wa loved the Karen nation above all others. But they transgressed his commands, and in consequence . . . we suffer as at present. Because Y'wa cursed us, we are in our present afflicted state and have no books."

Then a great hope seemed to light up his face as, looking toward the stars, . . . he exclaimed: "But Y'wa will again have mercy upon us, and again he will love us above all others. Y'wa will save us again. It is [because we listened] to the language of Mu-kaw-lee that we suffer."

Then followed . . . [an] impassioned recitation in the lyrical verse of his ancestors. . . . The old man . . . spoke with a native eloquence which can be felt, but not described:

"When Y'wa made Tha-nai and Ee-u, he placed them in a garden . . . saying, 'In the garden I have made for you seven different kinds of trees, bearing seven . . . kinds of fruit. Among the seven, one tree is not good to eat . . . . If you eat, you will become old, you will sicken, you will die. . . . Eat and drink with care. Once in seven days I will visit you . . .'

"After a time Mu-kaw-lee came to the man and woman and said, 'Why are you here?'

"'Our father put us here,' they replied.

"'What do you eat here?' asked Mu-kaw-lee.

"'Our Lord Y'wa has created food for us, food without limit.'

"'Show me your food,' said Mu-kaw-lee.

" . . . They pointed them out, saying, 'This one is astringent, this sweet, this sour, this bitter, this savoury, this fiery, but [as for] this tree, we know not whether it is sour or sweet. Our Father, the Lord Y'wa, said to us, 'Eat not the fruit of this tree. If you eat, you will die.'

" . . . Then Mu-kaw-lee replied, 'It is not so, O my children. The heart of your Father Y'wa is not with you. This is the richest and sweetest. . . . If you eat it, you will possess miraculous pow-ers. You will be able to ascend to heaven. . . . I love you, and I tell you the truth, and conceal nothing. If you do not believe me, do not eat the fruit. If you will each eat the fruit as a trial, then you will know all. . . .'"

In paragraphs that follow, the man, Tha-nai, refuses the enticement and walks away. The woman, Ee-u, lingers, succumbs to temptation, eats the fruit and then entices her husband, who also eats. Alonzo Bunker's translation continues:

" . . . The woman returned to Mu-kaw-lee and said, 'My husband has eaten the fruit.'

"[Mu-kaw-lee] laughed exceedingly, and said, 'Now O con-quered man and woman, you have listened to my voice and obeyed me.'

"The next morning Y'wa came to visit them, but they did not follow him with the singing of praises as usual. He drew near to them and said, 'Why have you eaten the fruit of the tree that I commanded you not to eat? . . . Therefore you shall grow old, and you shall become sick, and you shall die.'

". . . When Y'wa had cursed man, he left him. . . . In course of time sickness began to appear. One of the children of Tha-nai and Ee-u fell ill. Then they said to one another, 'Y'wa has cast us off. We cannot tell what to do. We must go and ask Mu-kaw-lee.'

"So . . . they went to him and said, ' . . . we obeyed your words, and ate. Now our child is ill. . . . What will you advise?'

"Mu-kaw-lee replied, 'You did not obey your Father, the Lord Y'wa. You listened to me. Now that you have obeyed me once, obey me to the end.'

Then the old prophet related, still continuing in the ancient verse of his people, how Mu-kaw-lee instructed them in the principal offerings to be made [for] various kinds of sickness. These offerings were to be made to his servants the nats [demons] who presided over certain diseases, as well as accidents.

He also told how Mu-kaw-lee instructed them to divine by the bones of a fowl, which became to these hillmen the guide to almost every act of life.

Alonzo Bunker also quotes a Karen "Song of Hope," expressing their longing for the eventual return of *Y'wa*:

At the appointed season Y'wa will come
. . . Dead trees will blossom and flower . . .
Mouldering trees will blossom and bloom again.
Y'wa will come and bring the great Thau-thee.
["Thau-thee" seems to be the name of a sacred mountain.]
Let us ascend and worship.

A second song of hope speaks of a king who will return:

Good persons, the good,
Shall go to the silver city, the silver town.
Righteous persons, the righteous,
Shall go to the new town, the new city.

Persons who believe their father and mother
Shall enjoy the golden palace.
When the Karen king arrives,
There will be only one monarch.
When the Karen king arrives,
There will be neither rich nor poor.[6]

Karen prophets, in spite of the ever-present and pervasive influence of Buddhist idolatry in Burma, constantly fortified their people against idolatry through proverbs such as the following:

O children and grandchildren! Do not worship idols or priests!
If you worship them, you obtain no advantage thereby,
While you increase your sins exceedingly.

Honoring one's parents was also a sacred obligation:

O children and grandchildren! Respect and reverence
your mother and father!
For when you were small, they did not suffer so
much as a mosquito to bite you.
To sin against your parents is a heinous crime.

Prophets of God among the Karen also emphasized man's duty to love God and one's neighbor:

O children and grandchildren! Love Y'wa, and never so much
as mention his name [lightly].
If you speak his name [lightly],
He goes farther and farther from us!
O children and grandchildren! Do not be fond of
Quarreling and disputing, but love each other.
Y'wa in heaven looks down upon us.
And if we do not love each other,
It is the same as if we do not love Y'wa.

Karen who violated the code were called to repentance with a promise of mercy from *Y'wa*:

> O children and grandchildren! If we repent of our sins,
> And cease to do evil—restraining our passions—
> And pray to Y'wa, he will have mercy upon us again.
> If Y'wa does not have mercy on us, there is no other one who can.
> He who saves us is the only one—Y'wa.

The importance of prayer was not overlooked:

> O children and grandchildren!
> Pray to Y'wa constantly By day and by night.[7]

The Karen people thus present a striking anomaly to theologians. Jesus, as far as the Gospel record tells us, commended the religious awareness of a comparative handful of Gentiles: a Roman centurion, a Syrophoenician woman, the Queen of Sheba, Naaman the Syrian, the widow of Zarephath, the people of Nineveh. Likewise Peter was startled by the unexpected piety of a Gentile called Cornelius (see Acts 10:34). The Karen race, however, confronts us with hundreds of thousands of individuals whose awareness of basic spiritual facts may have matched that of history's *average* Jew or Christian!

The piety of the pagans mentioned in the Bible, moreover, seems traceable in each case directly to Jewish influence. In two cases, the ministry of Jesus Himself was instrumental. But the Karen live 4,000 miles from Jerusalem. Granted, their name for God— *Y'wa*—suggests influence from the Jewish *Yahweh*, but no equivalents for Abraham and Moses, the second and third most important figures in Judaism, have been reported by compilers of Karen tradition. Surely Jewish influence would have emphasized Abraham and Moses.

Likewise, if Karen traditions trace back to, for example, Nestorian Christian influence of the eighth century, or to later Roman Catholic missionary contacts of the sixteenth, seventeenth or eighteenth centuries, one would expect some mention of an incarnation or a Redeemer dying for man's sin and rising from the dead.

Again, I have found no such concepts reported by students of Karen tradition.

And if we theorize that Jewish and/or Christian influence touched the Karen, but so fleetingly that only the basic concepts of God, creation and the fall of man registered with them, then we face a difficult question. How could so fleeting an influence leave such a deep and lasting impression on an entire people, especially when Buddhism and their own tribal spiritism so strongly opposed that influence over long periods of time?

History teaches that only very strong or very protracted influences can instill new religious concepts across cultural barriers, especially when other influences—Buddhism and spiritism in this case—are so contrary to those concepts.

Could it be that Karen beliefs about *Y'wa* predate both Judaism and Christianity? Did such beliefs spring from that ancient root of monotheism which characterized the age of the early patriarchs? The answer is almost certainly—yes!

By far the most amazing aspect of Karen monotheism was its frank acknowledgment of its own incompleteness. And in view of the natural worldwide tendency of most peoples to dislike and even distrust foreigners—especially if their color is different—the Karen anticipation that completeness would come to them via "white foreigners" is almost equally amazing. One of their hymns stated:

The sons of Y'wa, the white foreigners,
obtained the words of Y'wa.
The white foreigners, the children of Y'wa,
obtained the words of Y'wa anciently.[8]

During the 1830s, a Karen named Sau-qua-la gave an address before the English governor-general of Burma. He said that Europeans, the "white foreigners," were originally younger brothers of the Karen people! The Karen, as older brothers (rascals that they were), negligently lost their copy of *Y'wa's* book. The white brothers, on the other hand, carefully preserved their copy. As a result white people became "righteous" and are known as "guides to God." They also learned to sail in ships with "white wings," crossing oceans.[9]

Alonzo Bunker summarizes the tradition as follows: "The Deliverer [of the Karen] . . . was to be a 'white foreigner,' and was to come across the sea from the west with 'white wings' [sails] and bring Y'wa's 'white book.'"[10] Some versions of the tradition said the book would be of gold and silver.

The Karen nation was thus poised like an 800,000-member welcoming party, ready for the first unsuspecting missionary who approached them with a Bible and a message of deliverance from God. Whoever he proved to be, he was destined to enjoy one of history's greatest privileges!

Before we discover who the favored fellow was and what it took to get him on his way, let us scan the horizons of Burma and surrounding countries to see who else was waiting with bated breath for a message from the Almighty . . .

THE KACHIN

In the far north of Burma, another half-million red-turbaned, fiercely independent people called the Kachin also acknowledged their Creator. In their folk religion the Creator is called *Karat Kasang*—a benign supernatural Being "whose shape or form exceeds man's ability to comprehend." Sometimes the Kachin called him *Hpan Wa Ningsang*—the Glorious One Who Creates, or *Che Wa Ningchang*—the One Who Knows.[11]

Dr. Herman Tegenfeldt, Ph.D., who lived among the Kachin for about 20 years and learned their language, wrote: "Kachin animists do not offer sacrifice to Karai Kasang, for as one Kachin put it, 'Why should we? He never did us any harm.' Nor is there any custom of worshiping him. However, in times of extreme need, when sacrifices to the spirits have brought no relief, Kachins are known to cry out to this distant Great Spirit."[12] And the Kachin, like the Karen, believed that *Karai Kasang* once gave their forefathers a book which they lost. Kachin beliefs did not specify how the lost book would be returned to them, but apparently they were open to the possibility that it would one day be restored.[13]

Who would restore that lost book for the Kachin?

THE LAHU

Southeast of the Kachin and northeast of the Karen—in the region where Burma squeezes between China and Thailand to touch Laos along a 100-mile border—live about a quarter-million people called the Lahu.

For who knows how many centuries, the Lahu also had been haunted by a tradition which said that *Gui'Sha*—Creator of all things—had given their forefathers his law written on rice cakes! A famine came, and the forefathers ate the rice cakes for their physical survival. They rationalized this act by saying that *Gui'Sha*'s law would then be inside them! Indeed, the Lahu believed that a sense of *Gui'Sha*'s law was still within them because their forefathers ate the sacred rice cakes. They could not, however, obey their Creator perfectly until they regained the precise written form of His laws.

Like the Karen, the Lahu people had "prophets of *Gui'Sha*." Their mission—to keep expectation of help from *Gui'Sha* constantly alive in the hearts of the Lahu people. To this end the prophets recited proverbs such as the following: "If a man had ten armloads of walking sticks and walked until every walking stick was worn to a stub, he would still not find *Gui'Sha* [the true God]. But when the right time comes, *Gui'Sha* himself will send to us a white brother ["caucasophobes" may object, but history must be recorded as it happened] with a white book containing the white laws of *Gui'Sha*—the words lost by our forefathers so long ago! That white brother will bring the lost book to our very hearths!"[14]

Some Lahu even wore cords around their wrists symbolizing both their bondage to the nats and their need for a divinely appointed deliverer who would one day cut those cords from their wrists![15]

Among the Lahu mountains of Burma, China and Thailand, the stage for an awesome drama was set. But where were the white brothers who alone could cause the curtain on that stage to rise?

But that is not all . . .

THE WA

Scattered through mountains rising between the Kachin and Lahu domains lived another 100,000 tribesmen called the Wa. The Wa were headhunters—but not promiscuous ones! Just once a year—in the planting season—Wa tribesmen felt compelled by bloodthirsty nats to plant human heads in their fields along with their seeds—just to ensure a good crop, mind you! They didn't really want to hurt anyone.

Neighboring tribes always wished to leave for vacation when Wa were planting their crops, but unfortunately that was when they had to plant their crops too.

A benign influence, however, was at work within the folk religion of the Wa people. From time to time prophets of the true God, whom the Wa called *Siyeh*, arose to condemn headhunting and spirit-appeasement! One such prophet appeared during the 1880s. He was called Pu Chan by the Shan people (his Wa name is unknown today). Pu Chan persuaded several thousand Wa tribesmen in Pong Lai village and surrounding areas to abandon headhunting and spirit-appeasement. On what grounds? *Siyeh*, the true God, Pu Chan said, was about to send a long-awaited "white brother with a copy of the lost book." If he came close to Wa territory and heard that the Wa were practicing evil things, he might think them unworthy of the true God's book and turn away again! If that happened, Pu Chan warned, surely the Wa would never get another chance to have the lost book restored to them.

One morning Pu Chan saddled a Wa pony. "Follow this pony," he said to some of his disciples. "Siyeh told me last night that the white brother has finally come near! Siyeh will cause this pony to lead you to him. When you find the white brother, let him mount this pony. We would be an ungrateful people if we made him walk the last part of his journey toward us!"[16]

While Pu Chan's disciples gaped in astonishment, the pony started walking. Expecting the pony to stop at the nearest stream they followed it. Would it lead them to a "white brother"? The right one?

THE SHAN AND PALAUNG PEOPLES

Even some of the Buddhist peoples of southeast Asia manifested strong anticipation of a coming Messiah figure. Their Messiah, some sources claim, would come only as a "fifth manifestation of Buddha," called *Phra-Ariya-Metrai*—the Lord of Mercy. Nevertheless, the fact that such peoples longed for a "Lord of Mercy" shows their acknowledgement of a basic human need. The gospel speaks to that need, even though the "Lord of Mercy" proclaimed by the gospel is in no way a fifth manifestation of Buddha.

Apparently Buddhist scriptures quoted Gautama Buddha as saying: "After me will come *Phra-Ariya-Metrai*—the Lord of Mercy. When he appears, my followers must all follow him!" These scriptures, by one theory, were destroyed during times of war in the country of Laos,[17] yet the verbal tradition remains widespread not only in Laos and northern Thailand but also among the Shan and Palaung people of eastern Burma, where *Phra-Ariya-Metrai* is called, according to Alexander MacLeish, *Are-Metaya*.[18]

MacLeish writes concerning Shan and Palaung preoccupation with *Are-Metaya* that "no figure in all their religious horizon more quickly rouses their interest. In one of their books regarding [*Are-Metaya*] is found a verse [very similar to one] from Isaiah [saying in effect]: 'Every valley shall be exalted, and every mountain shall be made low, and the crooked shall be made straight, and the rough places plain,' and they expect Are-Metaya literally to fulfill this prophecy when he comes."[19]

MacLeish states further that the Palaung people, when they build a new home, always add an extra room to be held in reserve for *Are-Metaya*. The room is cleaned regularly even though members of the household never use it. At night it is always lit with a small lamp.[20] No one knew, apparently, when the "Lord of Mercy" would come or which dwelling he might approach seeking shelter. Thus all dwellings had to be ready at all times!

Just as every Jewish girl in Old Testament times hoped that *she* would be the mother of the Messiah, so also it seems that every Palaung household hoped to be one in which this Buddhist "Lord of Mercy" would one day take shelter!

THE KUI OF THAILAND AND BURMA

MacLeish states that Kui tribesmen, living along the Thai-Burma border, actually built houses of worship dedicated to the true God in anticipation of the time when a messenger from God would enter such places of worship with the lost book in His hand to teach the people! No idols were ever placed in such places of worship, but Kui folk would "gather and, in dim uncertain fashion, worship the great God above."[21]

THE LISU OF CHINA

Meanwhile, across the border in Yunnan Province of southwestern China, several hundred thousand Lisu hill-dwellers waited patiently for a white brother with a book of the true God written in the Lisu language! This is of special interest when one realizes that the Lisu language lacked even an alphabet, let alone printed material! No matter! The Lisu were convinced that one day *he* would come and give them a book of God written in their own language.

And when they received that book, they said, the Lisu would have a king of their own to reign over them (they had been subject to oppressive Chinese rule for many generations).[22]

We are not through yet . . .

INDIA'S NAGA AND MIZO

Beyond the mountains guarding Burma's northwestern border, 24 tribes of India's Naga race, totaling about 1 million people, were already equipped with a clear concept of "a Deity of highly personal character associated with the sky more than the earth," and who "stood above all others." In the Chakesang dialect, this God was called *Chepo-Thuru*—the God who sustains everything. In the Konyak dialect, his name was *Gtuang*.[23]

At least one of the 24 Naga tribes—the Rengma—specified that the Supreme Being gave His words to their forefathers by writing them on animal skins. But the forefathers did not take good care of the skins. Dogs ate them up![24]

The Naga also had prophets who arose among them from time to time. An author named Phuveyi Dozo, himself a Chakesang Naga, describes one prophet, a woman named Khamhimutulu, believed to have lived in the 1600s. The details of her prophecy reportedly reveal remarkable conformity to biblical principles and also to events which began to take place among the Naga at the beginning of the twentieth century. But we are getting ahead of our story . . .

Dozo also claims that Naga culture featured amazingly biblical customs such as the erection of memorial stones at special places, "first fruit" offerings, blood offerings, holy animal offerings, eating unleavened bread, ear-boring, keeping a "sacred fire" burning continuously, special regard for the number seven, harvest feasts and the blowing of trumpets after harvest!

And they never represented *Chepo-Thuru* with an idol!

Old Testament history shows that the Jews, even though they held the written law of God in their very hands, had a difficult time maintaining obedience to the law. Throughout most of their Old Testament history, the majority of Abraham's children *practiced idolatry*! Some even went to the extreme of *burning their own babies alive* before an idol named Moloch! The Naga had their problems too. Slavery was common among them, but then it was also practiced by some Christians as late as the mid-nineteenth century, and is still legal in many Moslem countries even today! Naga headhunting caused unnecessary loss of life. Opium smoking (introduced by the British to weaken the Naga militarily) sapped Naga initiative. Still, for an illiterate people, beset by temptations of spiritism on one hand and Hindu and Buddhist idolatry on the other, the Naga did surprisingly well to maintain so much awareness of God through so many centuries. What would the Naga have been like if they had not lost God's sacred writing?

Some 300 miles southwest of the Naga domain, and also straddling the India-Burma border, lived another 350,000 people called in India the Mizo. Burmese call them Lushai.

An author named Hminga, himself a Mizo, describes his people's awareness of *Pathian*—the one Supreme God: *Pa*, he says, means "father" and *Thian* has a possible interpretation of "holy." *Pathian* thus probably means "holy Father." Pathian was viewed as "the Creator of everything . . . a beneficent Being [manifesting] little concern for men." Hminga quotes a writer named McCall as saying: "The [Mizo] believed in the existence of one Supreme God, a God of all humanity and goodness."

Whereas the Kachin did not offer sacrifice to *Karai Kasang*—their name for the Supreme God—the Mizo did offer sacrifices to *Pathian*, and to Him alone!

Hminga states that a Mizo man named Darphawka had a prophetic and highly influential dream sometime during the nineteenth century: "In the night a voice spoke to him saying, 'A great light will come from the west and shine upon Mizoland. Follow the light, for the people who bring it will be the ruling race. . . .' [The prophet then said to his people:] 'This light may not shine in my lifetime, but when it comes, follow it! Follow it!'"[25]

Tegenfeldt quotes a writer named Hanson who claims that the Mizo people also possessed traditions of a sacred book. Pathian originally gave it to their forefathers, but they subsequently lost it.[26]

Ten entire peoples! All of them phenomenally equipped to understand the significance of the gospel of Jesus Christ if only they knew it existed! Ten peoples, totaling more than 3 million men and women! Ten peoples concentrated within a Texas-sized part of southeast Asia! Waiting . . . waiting . . . waiting . . . while *Y'wa*'s people in other lands let one century after another slip by! Then, at last, a new day began to dawn.

In 1817, a devout American Baptist missionary named Adoniram Judson disembarked near Rangoon, Burma, after a long sea journey from America. He had a Bible tucked under his arm, to be sure, but he possessed not the slightest inkling of the incredible significance that book held for more than 3 million people living within 800 miles of the dock on which he stood.

Judson found lodging in Rangoon. He learned the Burmese language with extreme care. At length, dressed in a yellow gown similar to those worn by Buddhist teachers in Burma, he ventured out into marketplaces and preached the gospel to Buddhist Burmese. Alas, Judson found little response. Often he struggled against an almost overpowering feeling of discouragement. Only after seven years of preaching did Judson find his first convert among the Buddhist Burmese!

All unknown to Judson, Karen people were passing daily by his home.[27] Often they were singing, as their custom was, hymns to Y'wa— the true God. If only Judson could have learned *their* language too, he would have been startled by the content of those hymns! And he almost certainly would have found more response for the gospel among humble Karen people than his fondest dreams could anticipate. All unaware of the awesome potential of the Karen, an often disconsolate Judson turned increasingly to the task of translating the Bible into Burmese, since he had so few converts to occupy his time with counseling.[28]

As it turned out, Judson's translation of the Bible into Burmese became foundational for all that his later-arriving colleagues were to accomplish among Burma's many minority peoples. If Judson himself had been caught up in a Karen-type response, he might never have found time to complete that translation!

Then, as Providence arranged, a rawhide-tough Karen man came to the very household where Judson stayed. He was looking for work to help him pay a debt. Judson arranged employment for him. That man was Ko Thah-byu. He had a violent temper and estimated that he had killed about 30 men during his former career as a robber![29]

Gradually Judson and other members of the household introduced Ko Thah-byu to the gospel of Jesus Christ. At first the Karen man's brain seemed too dense to grasp the message. Then a change took place. Ko Thah-byu began asking questions about the origin of the gospel and about these "white strangers" who had brought the message—and the book which contained it—from the West. Suddenly everything fell into place for Ko Thah-byu. His spirit received the love of Jesus Christ like dry land absorbing rain!

Around that time a newly recruited missionary couple, George and Sarah Boardman, arrived in Rangoon to assist Judson. George Boardman opened a school for illiterate converts. Ko Thah-byu had never dreamed of attending school. Now he quickly enrolled, for he was determined to learn to read that Burmese Bible as fast as Judson could translate it! To the amazement of Judson and Boardman, Ko Thah-byu manifested a total preoccupation with the Bible and its message.

For it had already dawned upon Ko Thah-byu that he was the very first among his people to learn that "the lost book" had actually arrived in Burma! Accordingly, he also accepted his own responsibility to proclaim the good news that virtually every Karen was waiting to hear. So when George and Sarah Boardman announced plans to launch a new mission in the city of Tavoy, in the panhandle of southern Burma, Ko Thah-byu said eagerly, "Take me with you!"

They took him. As soon as they arrived in Tavoy, Ko Thah-byu begged Boardman to baptize him. Boardman complied, and Ko Thah-byu set out immediately on a journey into the hills of southern Burma. Each time he came to a Karen village, he preached the gospel. And almost every time he preached, virtually every Karen within earshot responded with wonder! Soon hundreds of Ko Thah-byu's listeners came flocking down to Tavoy to see the "white brother" who had arrived at last with the lost book!

George and Sarah could barely believe their own eyes and ears! The entire hill country beyond Tavoy seemed to come alive with excitement! Soon Boardman found himself besieged with invitations from Karen villages to come and supplement Ko Thah-byu's ministry with more detailed teaching from "the Book of Y'wa." Meanwhile Ko Thah-byu kept on breaking new ground. Fording rivers, crossing ranges of hills, braving monsoon storms and bandits like those with whom he himself once roamed, he sought out one Karen village after another and proclaimed the good news! Finally he heard of the very village which—12 years earlier—had received a reportedly sacred book from the Muslim traveler. Ko Thah-byu urged Boardman to travel to the village and inspect the long-revered volume—to see if it was really a book about God. Mrs. Wylie's account, published in 1859, describes what happened when Boardman arrived in the village:

With a long train of followers, the chief appeared, bringing with him the sacred relic. The basket was opened, the muslin unrolled, and taking from its folds an old, tattered, worn-out volume, he reverently presented it to Mr. Boardman.

It proved to be the Book of Common Prayer and the Psalms, of an edition printed in Oxford. "It is a good book," said Mr. Boardman. "It teaches that there is a God in heaven, whom alone we should worship. You have been ignorantly worshiping this book. That is not good. I will teach you to worship the God whom the book reveals."

Every Karen countenance was alternately lighted up with smiles of joy, and cast down with inward convictions of having erred in worshiping a book instead of the God whom it reveals . . . [After hearing Mr. Boardman's subsequent teaching] the aged sorcerer who had been the keeper of the book for twelve years . . . perceived that his office was at an end. He relinquished the fantastical dress he had worn, and the cudgel which for so long had been the badge of his spiritual authority, and subsequently became a humble believer in the Lord Jesus Christ.[30]

"As the result of Ko Thah-byu's indefatigable labors," Mrs. Wylie wrote in another place, "many . . . Karen from . . . villages scattered over the mountains of Tavoy flocked in from the distant jungles, with curious interest to see the white teacher, and to listen to the wondrous truths he taught. Mr. Boardman found that notwithstanding their rude exterior they possessed minds susceptible to the most lively impressions, and remarkable teachableness of spirit."[31]

"When Mr. Boardman was able to visit the Karen in their own villages they received him with joy and respect, and hailed him as the one who, they believed, would show to them a more excellent way. From this time we find constantly in his journals entries like the following: 'A good number of Karens are now with us, and Ko Thah-byu spends night and day in reading and explaining to them the words of life. It seems as though the time for favoring this people [has] come.'"[32] Alleluia!

Meanwhile Jonathan Wade, also one of Adoniram Judson's newly arrived colleagues, was being swept off his feet by another explosively jubilant Karen response 200 miles north of Tavoy! Almost as quickly as Karen were converted and baptized, they became missionaries to spread the good news still further among their own people. Some of these Karen missionaries went to a place called Bassein—300 miles northwest of Tavoy—and preached there. Later when American missionaries arrived at Bassein, they found 5,000 Karen converts ready to be baptized!

Buddhist Burmese were amazed. "What," they kept asking, "is Christianity's secret? We Buddhists have tried for centuries to win the Karen to Buddhism—without success. Now, Christian missionaries are accomplishing in a few decades what we could not accomplish in centuries!"

Ko Thah-byu, meanwhile, left Tavoy—where he had aroused virtually the entire Karen population with the gospel—and cast himself like a firebrand into the midst of other tinder-like Karen populations in central Burma. Scarcely ever taking time for adequate rest, Ko Thah-byu burned himself out in a few years and died from his labors, but the fires he ignited in the midst of his people still blaze in Burma a century and a half later.

Still another of Judson's colleagues, Francis Mason, called Ko Thah-byu "The Karen Apostle" and wrote a book in his memory under that title. Mason's book ought to be reprinted for the edification of Christians in our day.

By 1858, tens of thousands of Karen Christians awakened to the realization that they were responsible to proclaim the good news of "the lost book restored" among other ethnic minorities of Burma besides themselves! Karen Christians from Bassein led the way into this new cross-cultural phase by sending teams of Karen missionaries—with an occasional American missionary as part of the team—to the 500,000 Kachin people living in Burma's northern hump.

The Karen missionaries were startled to find the Kachin also in possession of their own name for the Almighty—Karat Kasang—and not only that, the Kachin also believed that their forefathers had once possessed Karai Kasang's sacred writing! Like the Karen, the Kachin had rejected

Buddhist idolatry for centuries on the grounds that *Karai Kasang* would not approve. Also like the Karen, the Kachin responded to Christianity as the fulfillment of their own beliefs about *Karai Kasang.*

Within the next 90 years, some 250,000 Kachin people were added to the church of Jesus Christ!

Karen. Kachin . . . What of the Lahu and the Wa? Later, in the 1890s, the American missionaries commissioned one of their number, a certain William Marcus Young, to take the gospel to the Shan people in the eastern extremity of Burma. Karen missionaries, naturally, went with him. Young and his Karen colleagues established a base in Kengtung city, capital of the Shan region.

One day Young went to the marketplace to preach among the Shan people, most of whom were Buddhists. Young read Moses' Ten Commandments aloud. Then holding his Bible aloft—with the sun gleaming on its white pages—he began to preach about the laws of "the True God."

As he preached, Young noticed strangely garbed men gravitating toward him out of the throng in the market. Obviously, they were not Shan people. Later he discovered that they were Lahu men who had chosen that day to descend from distant mountains to trade their wares in the market of Kengtung. Soon they completely surrounded William Marcus Young. They stared incredulously at his white face, the white interior of the book in his hand, and listened to his description—in the Shan language—of the laws of God contained in that book.

Then, in an outburst of powerful emotion, the Lahu pleaded with William Marcus Young to follow them up into the mountains. In fact, they practically kidnapped him: "We as a people have been waiting for you for centuries," they explained. "We even have meeting houses built in some of our villages in readiness for your coming."

Some of the Lahu men showed him bracelets of coarse rope hanging like manacles from their wrists. "We Lahu have worn ropes like these since time immemorial. They symbolize our bondage to evil spirits. You alone, as the messenger of *Gui'Sha,* may cut these manacles from our wrists—but only after you have brought the lost book of *Gui'Sha* to our very hearths!"

Nearly speechless with awe, Young and the Karen missionaries went with them. What followed sounds like a nineteenth century Acts of the Apostles. Tens of thousands of Lahu became Christians. Young and his Karen colleagues could not satisfy Lahu demand for teaching, so Young pressed his two young sons—Harold and Vincent—into service as Bible teachers. Harold and Vincent wore Lahu garb from childhood. They joined in Lahu folk dances. They worked and laughed and played with the Lahu, and spoke Lahu even more fluently than English. Later Vincent translated the entire New Testament into beautifully colloquial Lahu.

In 1904, William Marcus, the Karen missionaries, and Harold and Vincent baptized 2,200 Lahu converts who had learned the basics of Christian faith. From then until 1936, when he died still in harness among the Lahu, Young saw at least 2,000 Lahu per year enter the waters of baptism. One year, he and his sons and his Karen colleagues baptized more than 4,500!

Hundreds of millions of Christians in Western lands are influenced by a stereotype of missionary work as a basically inefficient and unproductive enterprise. Most Christians think that 5 converts for every 20 years of missionary labor is the norm. Nothing could be further from the truth. Actually, missionary work has produced results so far beyond the expectations of even missionaries themselves that it boggles the mind to try to grasp its accomplishments in full perspective! Breakthroughs like those achieved by the Boardmans, the Wades and the Youngs are by no means uncommon in the experience of Christian missionaries. The "Sky-God," you see, knew they were coming into another of His many domains, and prepared the way for them. It's as simple as that!

The astonishing fact that missionary breakthroughs among the Karen, Kachin and Lahu tribes came *through* their respective folk religions, rather than in spite of them, has been completely lost upon some scholars. German anthropologist Hugo Adolf Bernatzik, for example, traveled through the Kengtung region in 1936-37, and later published a book called *The Spirits of the Yellow Leaves*. On page 188, Bernatzik begins a chapter called "Kengtung—Bemissioned"! Stunned and chagrined to find that "more than half of the mountain villages were now Christian," Bernatzik comments on this change, and on how he thinks it came about: "Kachin and Lahu congregated on Sundays in their 'churches,' thatched buildings on piles, to praise the God of the Christians."

Bernatzik scornfully suggests through his use of quotation marks that thatched buildings on piles cannot truly be considered churches. He little dreamed that the Lahu had erected similar structures in anticipation of the gospel long before it arrived! And if only he had inquired, he could have learned also that the God the Kachin and Lahu were worshiping in those churches was none other than *Karai Kasang*— Supreme God of the Kachin forefathers—alias *Gui'Sha* among the Lahu! Bernatzik continues: "The missionaries now stand here and proclaim a new God and expose the shortcomings and impotence of the old gods."

Bernatzik was not present, of course, when Lahu begged William Marcus Young to cut the old ropes from their wrists, symbolizing their escape from the bondage of the nats! Let us read more of Bernatzik's commentary:

> In . . . old Asia . . . in which there had for thousands of years been not only paganism but Brahma and Buddha, Mohammed and Confucius, Christianity today is inseparable from European civilization, which . . . will always be an alien element. . . .

What would Bernatzik think if he were alive today in "old Asia," where thousands of Karen, Kachin and Lahu congregations continue their thriving witness for Jesus Christ without the presence of even a single European missionary as advisor, let alone supervisor? How could such an opinionated man possibly even conceive of the fact that one of Asia's supposedly more acceptable religions—Buddhism—had failed miserably in its concerted attempts to win the conversion of these particular minority peoples of Burma, whereas Christianity—though not backed by the Burmese government—won their hearts in a few decades.

Bernatzik is typical of many intellectuals who predicted that Christianity, which they supposed was gaining ground in Asia and Africa by riding on the coattails of colonial governments, would quickly vanish from the third world as soon as nationalistic movements forced colonial governments to withdraw.[33]

In total defiance of such predictions, Christianity is now growing and spreading in the former colonial territories faster than it is even in America and Europe![34]

Bernatzik continues: "We could do nothing else but regard [the missionaries'] work from the point of view of the 'converted' people."

Anthropologists hostile to Christian missionary work are fond of suggesting—as Bernatzik does here through his use of quotation marks—that the conversion of far away peoples to Christianity is rarely genuine. Adherents of churches simply pretend to be Christians to satisfy the missionary, is the prevailing assumption. Actually, such peoples are fully capable of defying, abusing or even killing missionaries whenever they choose to reject the Christian way!

As I read on to see what is this view of the "converted" people, which Bernatzik promises to reveal to us, I am amused to find not a single quotation from a single supposedly hypocritical or browbeaten Kachin or Lahu church member! Bernatzik simply spoonfeeds us his own unresearched opinions and asks us to accept them as the "point of view of the 'converted' people." Then he reveals his unembarrassed paternalism in the following words: "These primitive men and women, moreover, are not psychologically in a condition to grasp [Christianity's] abstract ethic, and so do no more than accept immaterial superficialities, which in no way compensate for the destruction of their authoritative spirit world."

Poor Professor Bernatzik! Deceived by what Mrs. Wylie called the "rude exterior" of Kachin and Lahu people, he cannot even suspect the existence of the incredible spiritual dynamics which were even then at work in the Kachin/Lahu world—let alone understand those dynamics! He is typical of "intellectuals" who have been educated away from the discovery of such dynamics, rather than toward them.

In the rest of the chapter, Professor Bernatzik hires a non-Christian Lahu to lead him in search of Lahu villages which, he hopes, are still resisting the "coercions" of Christianity. The professor explains that his progress was greatly impeded because his non-Christian Lahu guide kept stopping en route to smoke opium. Finally the professor had to compromise with the enemy, so to speak, by hiring a Christian Lahu guide, so that his expedition could keep on schedule. The professor does not, of course, acknowledge any debt to the gospel of Jesus Christ for making it easier for him to find a Lahu guide not addicted to opium!

At last the professor found a non-Christian Lahu village. Its inhabitants, however, threatened his life and he had to seek still another, and another, and another—for every non-Christian Lahu village except one refused to welcome his party! And even the one village that welcomed him did so grudgingly. Bernatzik manages to remain philosophical about the situation by commending the non-Christian Lahu for their "independent spirit."

Apparently it never occurred to the professor to wonder how the missionaries were able to penetrate that same barrier of fierce independence.[35]

It was during the initial stage of the Lahu response to the gospel that Pu Chan, God's advocate among the headhunting Wa people, saddled the little pony and told his disciples to follow it in search of a "white brother bearing the book of Siyeh, the True God."

The pony led those amazed disciples over approximately 200 miles of mountainous trails and down into the city of Kengtung. Then it turned into the gate of a mission compound and headed straight for a well.

The pony stopped beside the well. Pu Chan's disciples looked in all directions, but could see no trace of either a white brother or a book.

Nelda Widlund, daughter of Vincent Young and granddaughter of William Marcus Young, told me in person what happened next. For she was raised on that very mission compound, and drank often from that very well. The details which follow form a treasured memory of the entire Young clan: The Wa tribesmen heard sounds in the well. They looked inside it and saw no water, but only two clear blue eyes looking up at them out of a friendly, bearded white face.

"Hello, strangers!" The voice—speaking in the Shan language—echoed out of the well. "May I help you?" William Marcus Young climbed out of the well, which was not yet in use (he was still in the process of digging it). As he brushed the dust from his hands and faced them, the Wa messengers asked, "Have you brought a book of God?"

Young nodded. The Wa men, overcome with emotion, fell at his feet and blurted out the message from Pu Chan. Then they added: "This pony is saddled especially for you. Our people are all waiting. Fetch the book! We must be on our way!"

Young stared at them. "I can't leave," he replied. "Thousands of Lahu come here almost daily for teaching. What shall I do?"

Young presented the situation to Lahu Christians. Together they decided to provide accommodation for the Wa men so that they could receive teaching in Kengtung and make trips back into Wa territory to teach their own people. By this means Pu Chan and thousands of his people became Christians without a single visit from William Marcus Young!

As a result of this arrangement, little Vincent Young—Nelda's father—grew up hearing the Wa language spoken around him almost as much as that of the Lahus! Later, as a teenager, Vincent made repeated journeys into the Wa mountains—an area avoided by travelers because of the Wa reputation for headhunting—and provided more detailed teaching "on location." As a result of such visits, Vincent learned the Wa language so thoroughly that he later followed up his translation of the Lahu New Testament with a second New Testament in Wa!

The Youngs and the Karen colleagues—in addition to baptizing about 60,000 Lahu—soon found themselves with another 10,000 baptized Wa converts, who in turn spread the gospel still further in eastern Burma and southwestern China!

At the end of my interview with her, Mrs. Widlund said, "Don, would you like to meet my father, Vincent Young, and see an ancient photo my grandfather took of that little Wa pony with the saddle on its back?"

"Do you mean to tell me your father is still living?" I exclaimed.

"He is now 80 years old, and lives in Mentone, California, just a few miles from here," she replied.

Later I met her at her father's humble dwelling in Mentone. She introduced me to Vincent Young himself, who in turn showed me—not only the photo of the pony—but also album after album of other ancient photos as well! There stood William Marcus Young at various stages of his life and ministry, and the Karen men and women who worked with him. I saw hundreds of Lahu and Wa standing in the shallows of rivers waiting to be baptized, while still other thousands blackened surrounding hillsides to observe the baptism. I drank in the triumph of it all until my heart felt ready to burst! Alleluia!

Does anyone doubt that God could cause a pony to lead those Wa men so unerringly over so great a distance? Surely the God who used a *star* to lead the Magi to the manger in Bethlehem could use a mere pony to find a certain well in Kengtung.

Across the border in southwestern China, an Englishman named James Outram Frazer, working under the auspices of the China Inland Mission, discovered the Lisu tribe, learned their language and began teaching the gospel among them. Encountering difficulties, Frazer crossed the border into Burma to see what he could learn about cross-cultural communication from American Baptist missionaries who, he had heard, were experiencing phenomenal success among peoples similar to the Lisu.

After an arduous journey, Frazer finally reached a Baptist outpost, but found it occupied only by Karen missionaries! Just as the apostle Paul used to "raid" Christian communities, taking from their midst the Timothys, Silases and Lukes he needed for his more wide-ranging ministry, so also Frazer "raided" the ranks of the Karen Christian community in Burma. He urged the Karen at that Baptist outpost to send one of their number with him for the spiritual benefit of the distant Lisu.

The Karen, in their typically admirable spirit, responded positively to his request. Frazer quickly returned to Lisuland with his new Karen helper, who also learned to speak Lisu.

Frazer, upon his return, translated the Gospel of Mark into the Lisu language. When published copies arrived from a mission print shop in Shanghai, Frazer traveled from village to village, reading from the Gospel of Mark.

Apparently Frazer at first was unaware that Lisu tradition had long before predicted the coming of a white-faced teacher who would restore to the Lisu a long-lost book of God in their own language. It seems likely that Frazer's Karen colleagues from Burma would certainly have been on the right wavelength to detect such a belief if Frazer himself missed it. In any case, the Lisu responded in large numbers to the gospel of Jesus

Christ, and many students of this case history believe that the ancient Lisu tradition, coupled with the presence of a Karen who could appreciate such a tradition in a special way, played a large part in generating the awesome movement of tens of thousands of Lisu men and women into the kingdom of God.

Burma, southwestern China, and then—eastern India! Few Christians in other parts of the world know that two entire states of predominantly Hindu India—Nagaland and Mizoram—boast a higher per capita ratio of baptized Christians than any other area of equal size anywhere in the world!

Churches in Nagaland, homeland of the approximately 2 million Naga people, embrace 90 percent of the entire population within their combined memberships![36] Mizoram, for its part, counts 87 percent of its entire population as church members.[37] Mizo Christians have distinguished themselves in the past by sending 400 of their own Mizo missionaries into predominantly Hindu areas of northern India.

Significantly, traditions of a lost book of God, combined with ancient predictions such as those uttered by the seventeenth century prophetess Khamhimutulu, played a major role in awakening Naga and Mizo populations to the meaning of the Christian gospel.

Travelers returning from such areas of eastern India frequently report that they were almost never out of sight of churches, and were almost always within earshot of prayer meetings and hymn singing!

Naga and Mizo Christians today still thank God that He gave them enough witness concerning Himself through their previous folk religions to keep them from yielding to the enticements of Hindu idolatry in India—just as Karen, Kachin, Lahu and Wa people had enough light to enable them to reject Buddhist idolatry in Burma and Lisu people had enough understanding to reject Taoism and Confucianism in China!

Had it not been so, the progress of the gospel among them would certainly have been much more labored.

Looking back over history, it appears that the Evil One's strategy has been to try to superimpose formal religions over folk religions before the gospel arrives—to prevent the native monotheism in the vast majority of folk religions from fulfilling its amazing role as an ally of the gospel.

This strategy has succeeded in the case of thousands of entire peoples who formerly adhered to folk religions. Due to Christianity's long delay in mounting a serious missionary outreach to them, the Sodom Factor eventually succeeded in neutralizing the Melchizedek Factor, as millions succumbed to pressures from Hinduism, Buddhism, Islam and other formal religions. Much of the receptivity which, by the grace of God, still awaited the gospel among the Karen et al, was dulled or muted in surrounding areas.

Nevertheless the task of winning adherents of the various formal religions to Christ is still not an impossible one! It is progressing, and we are steadily gaining momentum, as I shall detail in a later volume.

Epimenides, the Cretan prophet; Pachacuti, advocate of *Viracocha*; Kolean, the Santal sage; Pu Chan, the Wa prophet; Khamhimutulu, the Mizo prophetess; Worasa, Ethiopian seer—what are we to make of them? Does Scripture anticipate the existence of this unique class of God-fearers in the midst of otherwise pagan peoples?

I believe Scripture not only anticipates their existence, but even introduces us to at least six of them! I refer not only to Melchizedek, but also to Job and his four counselors: Bildad, Zophar, Elipaz and Elihu (see the book of Job).

These five God-fearers lived in the land of Uz. No one knows how they came to know God in Uz without the help of Abraham. In fact, no one even knows where Uz was!

Even Abraham was probably just such a person when Yahweh first spoke to him in Ur of Chaldea. Yahweh's subsequent selection of Abraham to father a special race of people for a special witness to the whole world was of course entirely unique. But the fact that Abraham personally knew the true God was not unique! As mentioned earlier, when Abraham arrived in Canaan, he found Melchizedek, king of the town named Salem, already serving as a priest of *El Elyon*—which was the Canaanite tribal name for God (see Gen. 14:18-20; Ps. 110:4; and Heb. 7:1-22).

Scripture even affirms, in fact, that Melchizedek was actually of higher rank in God's economy than Abraham! Abraham paid tithes to Melchizedek, and Melchizedek "blessed" Abraham, rather than vice versa. The fact that the writer of Genesis provides not the slightest explanation of how Melchizedek learned about *El Elyon* seems to indicate that the writer did not think it at all unusual that a person like Melchizedek should be found with such knowledge among the Canaanites!

Perhaps we too should not be surprised to find evidence of God-fearers living among pagan peoples in more recent times! Perhaps Jesus Himself referred to such when He said, "I have also other sheep which are not of this fold; I must bring them also" (John 10:16).

Peoples of the vague God and peoples of the lost book do not, however, tell us the whole story of God's Melchizedek Factor. Consider also the mystery of peoples with strange customs . . .

CHAPTER 3

Peoples with Strange Customs

Readers who are familiar with my first two books—*Peace Child* and *Lords of the Earth*—already have an idea of what I mean by "strange customs." For those who have not read *Peace Child*, for example, I give here a brief summary.

In 1962, my wife Carol and I, taking our eight-month-old son Stephen, traveled to New Guinea and lived as missionaries among the Sawi—one of nearly a thousand tribes living in New Guinea's 1,500-mile semicontinent. The Sawi proved to be one of five or six tribes on this planet who practiced *both* cannibalism and headhunting. Later three other children—Shannon, Paul and Valerie—were also born to us and spent their early years with us among the Sawi.

Our earliest attempts to communicate the gospel to the Sawi were frustrated by their admiration of "masters of treachery"—clever deceivers who could sustain a deception of friendship over a period of months while steadily "fattening" their victims with that friendship for an unsuspected day of slaughter!

Because of this unusual kind of hero-worship, the Sawi, listening to my early attempts to explain the gospel, mistook Judas Iscariot, Jesus' betrayer, for the hero of the story! Jesus, in Sawi eyes, was simply the dupe to be laughed at!

Suddenly Carol and I found ourselves grappling with two weighty problems. First, how could we make the real meaning of the gospel clear to people whose value system seemed so opposite to the New Testament ethic? Secondly, how could we be sure the Sawi were not fattening *us* with friendship for an unsuspected slaughter?

Praying for special help from God, we eventually found that the Sawi had a unique way of making peace and forestalling outbreaks of treachery. If a Sawi father offered his son to another group as a "Peace Child," not only were past grievances thereby settled, but also future instances of treachery were prevented—but only as long as the Peace Child remained alive. Our ready-made key of communication, then, was the presentation of Jesus Christ to the Sawi as the ultimate Peace Child, using Isaiah 9:6 John 3:16, Romans 5:10 and Hebrews 7:25 as the primary scriptural correspondents of the Peace Child analogy.

By this means, the meaning of the gospel did break through among the Sawi! Once they realize: that the one Judas betrayed was a Peace Child, they no longer viewed Judas as a hero. For to betray a peace child was, to the Sawi, the worst possible crime!

Since those days, approximately two-thirds of the Sawi people have, as they say, "laid their hands by faith upon God's Peace Child Jesus Christ," alluding to their former requirement that recipients of a peace child lay their hands individually upon the given son and say, "We receive this child as a basis for peace!"

Other peoples, however, possess equally strange customs which provide analogies to the gospel. The following chapters contain a number of examples. First, however, notice the following scriptural basis for finding and using such customs as eye-openers for spiritual truth.

Saul of Tarsus—who became Paul the apostle— had an advantage over Jews who spent all their days in Palestine. He had far more opportunity to observe Gentiles and their ways. Born in a predominantly Gentile city in a decidedly Gentile land, fluent in at least one Gentile language and a citizen of a truly cosmopolitan Gentile empire, Paul came to some interesting conclusions about Gentiles.

Here is one: Paul observed that Gentiles often behaved as if they were consciously conforming to the law of Moses, when in fact they had never heard of Moses or his law! *How can this be?* he wondered. Later the Spirit of God guided Paul to an amazing answer: "When Gentiles, who do not have the law, do by nature things required by the law, they are a law for themselves" (Rom. 2:14). In other words, the law expressed within pagan man's nature serves him as a sort of interim Old Testament. That is certainly inadequate, but it is ever so much better than having no law at all!

Paul continues: "They are a law for themselves, even though they do not have the law, since they show that the requirements of the law are *written on their hearts*, their consciences also bearing witness, and their thoughts now accusing, now even defending them" (vv. 14-15, emphasis added).

Paul was manifestly fair to Gentiles. He gave Gentiles, even the crudest ones, credit for possessing God-given moral sensitivity quite apart from Judeo-Christian revelation. Solomon, as we have seen, discerned that God "set eternity in the hearts of men" (see Eccles. 3:11). Now Paul adds that God has also written the requirements of His law in the same place!

Unregenerate man is doubly haunted! First he senses eternity, toward which he moves—finite speck that he is—as one strangely destined. Then he finds written upon his very heart a law which condemns them to miss his eternal destiny!

No wonder Paul wrote elsewhere, "Woe to me if I do not preach the gospel" (1 Cor. 9:16). Nothing else can end this double haunting of man!

Those of us who have extended the apostle's trails still further into Gentile domain have found his observation fulfilled in ways he himself

perhaps never anticipated. For example: One requirement of Moses'
law was a strange annual ritual involving two male goats. Both goats
were first presented to the Lord (see Lev. 16:7). The Hebrew high priest
then cast lots to select one of the two goats for an offering. Next he
slew the goat selected and sprinkled its blood upon "the atonement
cover" (Lev. 16:15).

What happened to the other goat?

The high priest laid his hands upon the second goat's head. Then he
confessed the sins of his people, symbolically placing them upon the second goat. A person appointed for the task then led this goat away from
the people and released it into the wilderness. Once the "scapegoat" had
vanished from view, the Hebrew people began praising Yahweh for the
removal of their sin.

When John the Baptist pointed to Jesus and exclaimed, "Look, the
Lamb of God, who takes away the sin of the world!" (John 1:29), he identified Jesus Christ as the perfect, personal fulfillment of Hebrew scapegoat symbolism. It took both animals to depict what Christ alone would
accomplish when He died for our sins. Not content merely to atone for
our guilt, He would also remove the very presence of our sin!

One sect has tried to develop a different interpretation. Agreeing
that the first animal foreshadows Jesus Christ, they insist that the scapegoat represents Satan. The author of sin, they reason, must ultimately
bear it away. This theory runs aground because it overlooks one detail
looming like a reef in its path. Both goats, not merely the first, had to be
presented before the Lord, implying that they had to be without defect,
as was customary in all Hebrew offerings.

Against this background, consider the following ceremony performed annually by certain clans among the Dyaks of Borneo.

THE DYAKS OF BORNEO

Dyak elders watch in a huddle as craftsmen apply finishing touches to a
miniature boat. The craftsmen hand the boat to the elders, who bear it
carefully to the edge of the river near their village, called Anik. While the
entire population of Anik watches, an elder selects two chickens from

the village flock. Checking to make sure both chickens are healthy, he slays one chicken and sprinkles its blood along the shore. The other chicken is tethered alive to one end of the deck of the little boat.

Someone else brings a small lantern, ties it to the opposite end of the deck and lights it. At this point each resident of the village approaches the little boat in turn and places something else, something invisible, upon the deck, midway between the shining lantern and the living chicken.

Ask a Dyak what he has placed between the lantern and the chicken and he will reply, "*Dosaku!*" (my sin).

When every resident of Anik has placed his or her *dosa* upon the little boat, village elders raise it carefully from the ground and wade out into the river. Then they release the boat into the current. As it drifts downstream, Dyaks watching from the shore grow tense. Elders standing chest-deep in the river hold their breath. If the little boat drifts back to shore, or hits a snag and overturns within sight of their village, the people of Anik will live under a pall of anxiety until the ceremony can be repeated next year!

But if the little boat vanishes around a bend of the river, the entire assembly will raise their arms toward the sky and shout, "*Selamat! Selamat! Selamat!*" (We're safe! We're safe!).[1]

But only until next year.

Jews had their scapegoat. Dyaks had their scapeboat.

Which one really could bear away sin? Answer: neither! The apostle who wrote the Epistle to the Hebrews said: "[Jewish] sacrifices are an annual reminder of sins, because it is impossible for the blood of bulls and goats to take away sins . . . . We have been made holy through the sacrifice of the body of Jesus Christ once for all" (Heb. 10:3-10).

If even God-appointed Jewish sacrifices were effective only as foreshadowers of something yet to come, then it goes without saying that the Dyak scapeboat also could not truly bear away sin. Does it then have no significance whatever? Not at all! The Dyak scapeboat embodies several valid concepts. Man needs to have his sin borne away! The removal of sin requires not only the death but also the living presence of something pure! The illumination of truth (symbolized by the shining lantern) is a necessary prerequisite for the removal of sin!

Who would have dreamed that Dyaks—once feared as headhunters—would turn up already pre-tuned to concepts beamed on this strongly parabiblical wavelength?

But caution: Buddhists in Cambodia also send little boats drifting down the Mekong River at certain times of the year. Dozens of these little lamp-bearing craft have been seen flickering on the Mekong at night. The Cambodian boats are intended either to bear away spirits of the dead or to take offerings of food to the dead. Their purpose has nothing to do with bearing sin away.

One must study the purpose behind any given custom before drawing conclusions about its potential relation to biblical concepts. Cambodian spirit-boats may originally have served a purpose similar to Borneo's "scapeboats." Ancestor worshipers over centuries, yielding to the Sodom Factor, may have changed the custom's original meaning so drastically that it no longer forms a bridge for biblical truth.

The good news that Christ became mankind's Sin-Bearer is one major component of the gospel. But it is not the whole news. The same Christ who bears away our sin also implants a new spirit within us lest we lapse endlessly back into the same offenses. Jesus said that all who receive this gift of a new spirit are "born again" (John 3:3).

The real meaning of "new birth" is difficult for most people to grasp. The first person Jesus talked to about new birth was a theologically sophisticated Jew named Nicodemus—a member of the Jewish ruling council, no less! Surely if anyone in Jerusalem should have been able to understand what Jesus meant by "new birth," it was Nicodemus. And yet . . .

As soon as Jesus said, "Unless a man is born again, he cannot see the kingdom of God," Nicodemus rebounded with the following naively literal, almost childish objection: "How can a man be born when he is old? . . . Surely he cannot enter a second time into his mother's womb to be born!" (v. 4).

If a seminary graduate like Nicodemus had that hard a time understanding what Jesus meant by new birth, surely "benighted Gentiles" around the globe will have a thousand times harder time understanding it! Right? Doesn't this indicate that Jesus' teachings may be, quite frankly, far above the heads of most people?

Not at all!

Let's take one of the toughest cases on earth . . .

NEW GUINEA'S ASMAT PEOPLE

Look at New Guinea on a globe. Its very shape seems to flash a warning: "Approach at Your Own Risk!" For New Guinea looks almost exactly like a huge tyrannosaurus basking, mouth agape, on the equator of our world.

The warning bears heeding. The list of travelers whose lives have been gobbled by that 1,500-mile-long reptile-shaped island reads like a veritable *Who's Who!* Check under *R.* That's right—the tyrannosaurus did not even respect a name as august as Rockefeller, as I shall explain later.

Mountain peaks—protruding like armor platelets from that reptile's spine—range the entire length of New Guinea. Several dozen summits surpass even the Matterhorn in height! But to the south extends a swamp so vast it reduces Florida's Everglades to a backyard duck pond by comparison. Thirty thousand square miles of rain forest! Serpentine rivers, many of them clogged with floating islands of grass. All sustained by 22 feet of rainfall annually!

Nearly a thousand tribes inhabit New Guinea. And one of them—the Asmat—has chosen to make its home in the wettest, densest, most humid, most disease-ridden part of that swamp.

Anthropologists have a rule of thumb. It states that headhunters, wherever you find them, will not also practice cannibalism. Cannibals, conversely, will not engage in headhunting. These two customs, says the rule of thumb, are mutually exclusive. You may find one or the other, but never both in any one culture.

The Asmat, unfortunately, never heard of the rule. Not content merely to save the skulls of their victims as trophies, they also devoured their victims' flesh as well![2]

The Asmat had still other interesting uses for parts of human bodies. Sometimes an Asmat man would prop a human skull under his head for a pillow. Asmat children played with human skulls as toys. Some warriors sharpened human thighbones to a point and used them as daggers. Human jawbones sometimes served as neck ornaments. And human blood formed the glue the Asmat used to bond black lizard-skin drumheads on their drums!

When you read this description of the Asmat, beware lest you be tempted to think of them as somehow not truly human. For if people who do such things must be considered subhuman, then what shall we say of the Celtic, Norse and Anglo-Saxon tribes from whom many who read this book are descended?

According to Dr. Ralph Winter, missiologist, headhunting occurred among Celtic tribes in Ireland. And brawny Anglo-Saxon denizens of forests in northern Europe drank, he says, out of human skulls as late as A.D. 600!

It was the gospel of Jesus Christ which made the difference for Celts, Norsemen and Anglo-Saxons. And that is exactly what it will take for Asmat headhunter-cannibals! All someone has to do is go to live among the Asmat and communicate the gospel as effectively as someone once communicated it to Celts, Anglo-Saxons and other tribes of Northern Europe!

Surely that is not too much to ask. Jesus said, "Freely you have received, freely give" (Matt. 10:8).

It is not—*indeed* it is not—too much to ask. But neither is it an easy thing to accomplish. And yet, part of the difficulty is only apparent. Picture yourself as one assigned to this very task . . .

You have located yourself in a small thatch-roofed home beside an Asmat village called Ochanep. In October, 1961, New York Governor Nelson Rockefeller's son, Michael, vanished from the face of the earth somewhere within a few miles of your home. You have heard speculation that your Asmat neighbors may have been the agency which caused Michael to disappear. And yet, to your relief, the Asmat appear friendly enough.

Not only have they helped you build your home, but also they provide you daily with plenty of fish, shrimp and wild pork in exchange for fish line, fishhooks, razor blades, matches, salt, knives, machetes or axes.

Others take time to help you learn their language. At first, Asmat strikes you as an impossible mixture of gibbles, gabbles and gobbles. Eventually, however, the good sense of it emerges. You begin to feel the excitement of breaking through!

Then come the shocks. Besides combining headhunting and cannibalism, Asmat men sometimes dehumanize their own wives by forcing them to cooperate in public wife-trading practices. At other times, they venerate dead relatives by handling decomposing flesh of their corpses.

Trying to persuade Asmat to change their minds about such things seems about as easy as changing a tire on a big Mack truck while it is rolling downhill. Trying to fix the gospel in their minds is like trying to nail Jell-O to a tree.

Eventually, as water presses through cracks in the hull of a boat, discouragement forces its way in and swamps your initial optimism. Your depression increases when you begin receiving letters from fellow missionaries in other parts of New Guinea—letters that say, "Rejoice with us! We have already baptized 6,000 believers in this valley alone! Another 2,000 are enrolled in literacy classes!"

Grimly you mutter, "Sounds like they need help up there!" Soon you pen a letter to the field administrator of your mission, requesting transfer to some more responsive people of New Guinea. "I have been trying everything among these people and have gotten nowhere," you advise. "Apparently this is not God's time to move among them."

Since, however, there is no mailbox in Ochanep (not to mention a post office), you cannot mail your letter until the next time a missionary pilot lands a float plane on the river near your home, providing your only link with the outside world.

As you lay your letter on the coffee table, an uproar breaks out in Ochanep. You run to your front door and glance toward the village. Hundreds of Asmat men, women and children throng down from their elevated longhouses and line up along the shore of the river. All are gazing excitedly downstream.

You yourself dash to the shore and look downstream. To your utter horror, the river in that direction is black with canoes of Basim people—deadly enemies of your Ochanep neighbors! You hear them coming.

Scraping their paddles against the sides of their dugouts. Thumping their feet upon the floor of their dugouts in accompaniment to that scraping. And venting deep chested shouts in accompaniment to both that thumping and that scraping!

You shudder. For you know that their paddles can double as spears. And that black palmwood bows and hundreds of cane-shafted arrows line the inside walls of their dugouts. And that many warriors in those canoes also carry human thighbone daggers stuck through their arm bands.

"There's going to be a blood bath right here in front of my home," you gasp.

"Not so!" replies a cheerful Asmat boy standing nearby. "Today they are not coming to make war. They are coming to make peace!"

"I hope it works!" you mutter tensely.

As you watch from what you hope is a safe distance, the Basim canoes pull abreast of Ochanep and veer shoreward. The canoes lodge against the mud bank, but the men in them keep coming! Right up onto the shore! Sticking their paddles upright in the mud, they form a solid mass and begin leaping up and down, shouting in utter exhilaration. This action triggers like response from the people of Ochanep.

Suddenly men representing both the Ochanep and Basim factions move, unarmed, toward each other and mingle on a small grassy knoll. Oddly, each man carries a mat rolled under his arm. Moments later, these mutual enemies spread their mats upon the grass and lie facedown upon them, side by side, for all the world like sunbathers on a crowded beach.

Then the wives of the reclining men advance shyly to the same knoll. "Oh, no!" you exclaim in revulsion. "Not another wife-trading orgy!"

This time you are mistaken. Each shy Asmat wife takes a position standing beside her reclining husband, ankles apart, with one foot tucked under his chest and the other under his hip. Then elders of both faction bring children to the knoll and instruct them to get down on their hands and knees and squirm forward across the backs of the reclining fathers. In the process, the children also pass between the knees of the mothers.

As each Basim child comes through that living passageway, he or she is picked up by men and women from Ochanep and rocked like a newborn baby. Others bring water and bathe him or her, as if cleansing birthstains from an infant. Ochanep children, conversely, are handled in the same manner by Basim people.

Next, decorated with palm-fiber tassels and sea shells, the children become the focus of several days of joyful celebration. Each night, adults rock them to sleep. Women coo lullabies in their ears. Then the children return freely to their own families in their own villages.

From that time forward peace ensues! Food-gathering parties may now forage deeper into sago swamps without fear of ambush. Basim and Ochanep men and women exchange not merely gifts, but even their very names, symbolizing unity and mutual trust.[3]

Meanwhile, a fierce struggle rages within you, the spectator. Your prejudice exclaims, "Bah! Repulsive pagan custom! Who cares about such things!" Your curiosity, however, makes a vital observation. Whatever it means, the custom conveys a dynamism capable of altering the behavior of Asmat people—the very thing you hope to achieve for a biblical purpose!

Let's hope your curiosity wins! If it does, you will begin asking questions. Before long, you will discover that the passageway formed by the backs of the fathers and the ankles of the mothers represents a communal birth canal! Children passing through are considered reborn into the kinship system of their enemies! By means of these reciprocally reborn children, both warring factions become one extended family, thus securing peace.

Suddenly realization comes crashing in upon you. For who knows how long, this peace-making ceremony has been impressing a valid principle upon Asmat minds—genuine peace cannot come through mere verbal agreement. It requires a new birth experience!

Scratching your noggin, you ask yourself, *Now where have I heard that before?*

Doggedly you sniff out Asmat nouns and verbs which capture the subtle meanings you need. Faithfully you practice until you can conjugate those verbs correctly through every tense of the Asmat indicative mood.

Then, trembling with excitement, you fit your toes into the notches of an Asmat stairpole and climb up into the longhouse of a man called Erypeet.

Erypeet sits naked on a mat, munching contentedly on a stick of toasted beetle grubs. Inviting you to sit on a nearby mat, he offers you a stick of toasted beetle grubs! You take it politely and lay it on the mat beside you—to be eaten after you return home, of course!

"Erypeet," you begin, "I was fascinated when I saw how you of Ochanep made peace with the Basim people. Once I too was at war, Erypeet. I was at war not with mere men, but with my own Creator. The shadow of that war darkened my life for many moons. Then one day a messenger from Creator approached me. 'My Master has prepared a new birth,' he said. 'You can be reborn within Him, and He can be born in you. Then you will be at peace with my Master.'"

At this point Erypeet lays down what remains of his stick of toasted beetle grubs and exclaims, "What! Do you and your people have a new birth too?" Erypeet is startled to find that you, an ignorant foreigner, an alien, an outsider, are actually sophisticated enough to even think in terms of new birth. He thought that only an Asmat could grasp a concept so profound!

"Yes, Erypeet," you reply. "We have a new birth too!"

Erypeet asks, "Is your new birth like ours?"

"There are some similarities, my friend; and there are some differences. Let me tell you about them!"

What chance is there that Erypeet may interrupt, saying, "Wait! How can a man be born when he is old? Can he enter the second time into his mother's womb and be born?"

Virtually none. For when it comes to reasoning about mankind's need to experience new birth, Erypeet—naked, illiterate, a headhunter-cannibal—has an advantage Nicodemus the Jew did not possess!

And what of that letter you wrote to the field administrator? What of that request for a relocation to some other part of New Guinea where the potential for response to the gospel is greater?

"Oh, that!" I hear you reply. "Well, you see, I've changed my mind. No way will I leave the Asmat now! I'm going to hang in here and see what the

Spirit of God may do in the hearts of these people when He reveals to them that Jesus Christ has a *real* new birth waiting for them, not just a symbolical one!"

Somehow I thought you would change your mind—once you understood.

THE YALI AND THE HAWAIIANS

What did 35,000 black-skinned Yali cannibals in central New Guinea have in common with the Jews? And also with brown-skinned Polynesian people living 5,000 miles away in the Hawaiian Islands?

Let the following narrative illustrate.

"Erariek, tell me a story," I asked, holding my ballpoint pen poised for note taking. Erariek, a 25-year-old Yali, grinned. He was obviously pleased by my interest in his people. Then his eyes lit up as an old memory returned—an adventure involving his own brother, Sunahan, and a friend named Kahalek. Erariek cleared his throat and described how the two men went to gather food early one morning.

Just as they began digging sweet potatoes from their garden, Sunahan and Kahalek heard an arrow zing past them. In the next instant a second arrow struck Kahalek. Glancing over their shoulders, the two food gatherers saw a large group of raiders emerging from ambush. The gleam in each raider's eyes told Sunahan and Kahalek that these enemies from across the Heluk River fully expected to feast on human flesh that very day—Sunahan's and Kahalek's flesh!

Dropping their digging sticks, Sunahan and Kahalek grabbed their bows and arrows and bolted for their lives.

At this point I expected Erariek to tell me that Sunahan and Kahalek fled up a steep trail toward the safety of their village on a ridge high above the garden area. Instead he told me that they turned from the trail and fled across their gardens toward a low stone wall. Just before they reached the wall more arrows struck already-wounded Kahalek. He fell just outside the wall and lay dying.

Sunahan, however, leaped over the wall, whirled around, bared his chest at his enemies and laughed at them. The raiders, after snuffing out

Kahalek's life with still more arrows, decided not to try to transport his body away for cannibalistic purposes—avengers from the village above were already swarming down the mountain. Carrying Kahalek's corpse would slow the raiders in their escape.

The raiders fled, leaving Sunahan without a scratch.

I nearly dropped my ballpoint pen! "Why didn't they kill Sunahan?" I asked. "He was standing right there!"

Erariek smiled condescendingly, "Don, you don't understand. Sunahan was standing *inside* the stone wall."

"What difference did that make?" I queried.

"The ground inside that stone wall," Erariek explained, "is what we Yali call an *Osuwa*—a place of refuge. If the raiders had shed one drop of Sunahan's blood while he stood within that wall, their own people would have punished them with death when they reached home. Likewise, although Sunahan held weapons in his hands, he dared not release an arrow at the enemy while standing within that wall. For whoever stands within that wall is bound to work violence against no man!"

You could have knocked me over with a feather!

Readers will find many more details about Erariek and the incredible saga of the Yali tribe in my book *Lords of the Earth*.[4] Now I must answer the question: What does all of this have to do with the Hawaiian people, 5,000 miles distant from rain-chilled Yali valleys in New Guinea?

No one knows when the Hawaiians first dedicated the sacred precinct called *Pu'uhonua-o-honaunau* for its special purpose. Archaeologists believe that King Keawe-ku-i-ke-káai—around A.D. 1500—built a temple on the site and surrounded it with a 10-foot-high stone wall, much of which still stands. Two subsequent temples were added during the following century.

Pu'uhonua-o-honaunau still stands on the western shore of Hawaii about six miles south of the monument commemorating the death of English explorer Captain James Cook.

Pu'uhonua-o-honaunau was not just another temple. It was a place of refuge for "defeated warriors, noncombatants, or taboo breakers" who reached its boundaries ahead of their pursuers (according to a National Park Service Brochure). Getting inside King Keawe's ancient wall was no mere game of prisoner's base. It meant life itself.

Any fugitive who entered found a shelter already built for him! A garden and a grove of coconut palms provided sustenance. A spring bubbled with fresh water. A stretch of ocean beach invited him to swim and to fish!

And *Pu'uhonua-o-honaunau* was only one of a network of perhaps 20 such "cities of refuge" scattered throughout the Hawaiian island chain!

Yali. Hawaiians. But what does this have to do with Jews and their traditions?

Once the Hebrews—forefathers of the modern Jewish people—entered the Promised Land, Joshua their leader followed an earlier directive given by God through Moses. He designated six Hebrew cities—three on each side of River Jordan—as "cities of refuge."

Their purpose? To provide shelter for individuals fleeing from any threat of death by violence (see Josh. 20 and 21). Jewish historians tell us that roads leading to the cities of refuge were generally the straightest roads in Palestine. Bridges along those roads were kept in good repair. The six cities themselves were all built on high ground so that a fugitive could see them clearly, even from a great distance.

Once a fugitive entered a Hebrew city of refuge, he was safe until a high priest arbitrated his case. Depending upon the results of the arbitration, the fugitive might be handed over for execution or released as a free man.

Hebrew poets and prophets from that time forward did not waste the poignant imagery and spiritual significance of the "place of refuge." For example, King David the psalmist wrote, "In you, O Lord, I have taken refuge; let me never be put to shame" (Ps. 31:1).

If the high priest decided, after arbitration, to hand the fugitive back to his prosecutors for execution, the fugitive was said to be "put to shame." King David, sensing that his own righteousness would not be sufficient to win his case before God, continues by pleading, "Deliver me in *your* righteousness" (Ps. 31:1, emphasis added). And that is what Jesus Christ, through the gospel, promises to do—deliver penitent refuge-seekers on the basis of *His* goodness, not theirs. They must be sure, however, to seek that refuge in Him, not just anywhere! The writer of the Epistle to the Hebrews fastened upon the same eternal principle of divine mercy when he wrote: "We . . . have fled for refuge to lay hold upon the hope set before us" (Heb. 6:18, *KJV*).

Note God's apparent strategy. First He instilled the "place of refuge" concept into Hebrew culture. Then He guided David and other biblical writers to appropriate "place of refuge" imagery as eye-openers both for Hebrews and for peoples like ourselves. May He not also have caused Yali tribesmen and Hawaiians to obey "by nature" this further requirement of "the law written on their hearts"? If so, then surely it must be His purpose that we, in turn, use the imagery afforded as eye-openers for them.

THE CHINESE AND THEIR WRITING SYSTEM

Early missionaries to China faced a formidable obstacle. They had to learn the Chinese writing system. As Westerners, accustomed to writing with European alphabets of approximately 26 letters, they gasped! Chinese writing, they found, used a system based upon 214 symbols called "radicals."

They gasped again when they learned that those 214 radicals—enigmatic enough in themselves—combine to form between 30,000 to 50,000 ideographs.

It was enough to make even the most patient saint gripe! Why on Earth would the sovereign God permit any people to develop a writing system so "radical"? Didn't it matter to God that Chinese writing placed an almost impassable barrier in the way of communicating the gospel to one-quarter of mankind?

One day, however, one of the missionaries stopped complaining. He was studying a particular Chinese ideograph, the one which means "righteous." He noticed that it contained an upper and lower part. The upper part was simply the Chinese symbol for a *lamb*. Directly under the lamb was a second symbol, the first person pronoun *I*. Suddenly he discerned an amazingly well-coded message hidden within the ideograph: *I under the lamb am righteous!*

It was nothing less than the heart of the gospel he had crossed the ocean to preach! Chinese were startled when he called their attention to the hidden message. They had never noticed it, but once he pointed it out, they saw it clearly. When he asked, "Which lamb must we be 'under' to be righteous?" they had no answer. With consummate delight he told them of "the Lamb that was slain from the creation of the world" (Rev. 13:8), the same "Lamb of God who takes away the sin of the world" (John 1:29).

He shared his discovery with fellow missionaries and soon they in turn began uncovering still other spiritual messages encoded within the 4,000-year-old ideographs! Chinese language study suddenly became the most exciting adventure they had ever experienced!

Another example: The Chinese symbol for a boat embodies a vessel with eight people inside it. Eight people? Noah's ark bore exactly eight people to safety.

The radical meaning *man* is a figure shaped like an upside down *y*. The ideograph meaning *tree* is a cross with the symbol for *man* superimposed upon it! And the symbol for *come* calls for two other smaller symbols for *man* to stand on either side of the tree with the greater man superimposed upon it. Some students of Chinese writing claim that the two smaller human figures collectively mean *mankind*. If so, the ideograph meaning *come* seems to carry a code that says: "Mankind come to the man on the tree."

For careful study of several other spiritually pregnant Chinese ideographs, I refer readers to C. H. Kang and E. R. Nelson's recent book on the subject, listed in the bibliography. Not all researchers agree on the exact interpretation of each and every symbol. Nevertheless, Chinese people themselves (and many Japanese, for Japan uses virtually the same writing system) have been intrigued by interpretations which missionaries have suggested to them. Even when theories are nonconclusive, the mere discussion of them may be sufficient to communicate spiritual truth to unbelievers.

I have found in my research that many Chinese and Japanese pastors themselves consider the use of these various symbols a valid entrée to the minds of their own people.

One missionary, returned from China, told of a Chinese soldier who approached him, bristling with hostility. The missionary sketched some of the aforementioned symbols on a pad and pointed out their "hidden" meanings. The soldier's eyes opened wide. "I was told," he exclaimed, "that Christianity was a foreign devil's religion! Now you show me that the writing system of my own country preaches it!"

NORTH AMERICAN INDIANS

From Alaska to Panama and from Baja California to Labrador—it keeps showing up in one way or another.

The Sacred Four!

Virtually all tribes talk about the four directions and the four winds. Navaho point to their four sacred mountains. The Sioux conduct their rainmaking dance with four sets of four horses each, each set of horses painted the same color—four colors in all. Many tribes use four-armed crosses or swastikas, or a four-sided design called "God's Eye" to denote the Sacred Four. Some Indian elders, when teaching tribal ways to children, customarily arrange their lesson material in sets of four. Indian children, consequently, soon find it easier to remember things that come in sets of four.

Ask a number of Indian "lore-keepers" to describe the essence of the Sacred Four and a consensus of their replies will run something like this: When the Great Spirit (*Wakan Tonka* to the Sioux, *Saharen-Tyee* to the Chehalis and so on) created the world, he ordained the Sacred Four to maintain order. Thus the Sacred Four are not four gods or four demons, but four order-sustaining principles which prevent everything from collapsing in chaos.

Ask Indians to articulate the Sacred Four individually and you will draw a blank. If ever Indians knew how any one differed from the other three, the knowledge has long since been lost. Indians speak of them collectively, and no other way.

Significantly, a number of missionaries to various North American Indian tribes have reported, without realizing why, that whenever they teach the *Four Spiritual Laws* (Campus Crusade for Christ), Indians sit up and listen! Revivals have even broken out when such material is presented in depth, especially by someone whom Indians have learned to respect.

Ed Malone, pastor of the Whittier Christian Fellowship in California, makes yearly visits to Navaho areas to teach budding young Indian pastors. Pastor Malone's comment: "It is amazing how much interest a four-point sermon generates among Navaho!"

Picture a teacher holding a *Four Spiritual Laws* booklet in front of a group of Indians, saying, "Here are four spiritual laws. Disobey them and your life is headed for chaos. Obey them, and God will bring stability and order into your life, your family, your job, your future . . . ."

Ancient Indian beliefs about the Sacred Four hang like an invisible sounding board behind the teacher, adding special weight and gravity to every word.

Is the Sacred Four concept a mere fiction? Or could it have some validity? Does the Bible hint at the existence of a God-ordained Sacred Four upholding order in the universe?

I believe the answer to all of these questions is yes! Consider the evidence:

1. The 12 tribes of Israel, heading for the Promised Land, always camped in 4 groups of 3 tribes each. Banners were allocated not to each of the 12 tribes but to each of the four groupings.
2. Jewish altars were designed with four "horns" projecting from the four corners. Sacrifices, to be valid, had to be literally tied to all four horns, not merely laid upon an altar.
3. The New Testament gives us four Gospels.
4. Jesus died upon a four-armed cross.
5. The Apocalypse speaks of four horses of four different colors, with four different riders.
6. Finally, the Bible seems to teach implicitly that all of reality is divided into four levels of a cosmic echelon. The highest level is reserved for God, the Sovereign over all things. Below God lies the citizen level, the rightful place for all beings created in the image of God. Below the citizen level we find what we may call the denizen level—reserved for flora and fauna. Finally, on the lowest level, matter, energy and the laws of nature find their place.

Nothing exists that does not fit into one of these four levels of the cosmic echelon. Further, as long as each entity remains within its appointed level, order prevails! Sin occurred only when a being created to exist on the citizen level sought to climb out of his slot and usurp God's rightful place as Sovereign of all.

Truly, there may be much more to the Indian concept than meets the mind at first consideration.

CHAPTER 4

Scholars with Strange Theories

In the preceding chapters, I have spoken only of patriarchs, apostles and Christian missionaries encountering the worldwide phenomenon of what could perhaps be called "native monotheism." By now readers are surely asking, "Are not scholars of the secular academic world aware of the phenomenon?" And if they are, what sense do they make of it?

The answers to these questions form one of the most interesting chapters in the early history of anthropology and ethnology.

First, some background.

The nineteenth century was a period characterized by a passionate search for the origins of anything and everything. Much of the excitement arose from a general expectation that a theory which had been incubating for centuries in certain schools of philosophy might at last provide a key to all mysteries. The theory was labeled variously as "materialistic transformism," "development" or "evolution," with the latter term winning prominence.

When Charles Darwin applied and extended evolutionary principles to show how diverse biological forms could have emerged from simpler forms, the excitement increased. Other thinkers, working more or less concurrently with Darwin, hoped that principles of evolution would enable them to unlock mysteries of another kind of phenomena—the origins of human society, culture and religion. How did this particular group of scholars propose to explain the origin of something so complex as religion, for example, on an evolutionary model?

First, they dismissed the Bible's claim that the first religion to appear on Earth was a monotheistic faith—a faith which the one true God has confirmed since antiquity with successive revelations.

Nor did they accept another biblical insistence, that spiritism and polytheism in all their forms are "false" religions resulting from man's perverse attempts to remold the original "true" religion after his own misguided preference. In other words evolutionists erased distinctions between "true" and "false" religion as scientifically meaningless. Lumping all religions in the same crucible, they advanced a bold hypothesis: that the very religions the Bible calls "false" originated first!

For example, an Englishman named Edward B. Tylor theorized, in a two-volume work called *Primitive Culture: Researches into the Development of Mythology, Philosophy, Religion, Art and Custom*, that the idea of a human "soul" must have been the natural seed thought from which all other religious concepts evolved.[1] Ancient savages, Tylor suggested, imagined that they had "souls" while wondering at two groups of biological problems: sleep, ecstasy, illness and death on one hand, and dreams and visions on the other. The idea of "soul" was reinforced as savages noticed their reflections in water or their own shadows—apparent extensions of themselves. Dreaming, they saw themselves in places where, upon waking, they knew they had not been—at least not in their *bodies*.

Once primitives got used to thinking of themselves as possessing souls, Tylor continued, it dawned upon them that other entities—animals, trees, rivers, mountains, the sky and even forces of nature—might be similarly endowed. Thus did spiritism (Tylor called it "animism") come to birth—the first religion!

Ages later, said Tylor, a new phenomenon emerged in some human societies—stratification of classes! Human aristocracies ruling over peasants suggested aristocracies of "gods" ruling over run-of-the-mill souls and spirits. Thus polytheism, in Tylor's model, emerged from spiritism—but only where the social phenomenon of stratification of classes prompted it!

Still later, some human aristocracies experienced a further metamorphosis: one aristocrat was fortunate enough to be exalted above his peers as a monarch. Once again, theologically precocious minds projected this latest social development over their vision of the supernatural world. Result: One member of the local pantheon of gods began to gain stature above his fellow deities as a budding "supreme god." Thus monotheism, said Tylor, gradually evolved out of polytheism—but only in areas where the social phenomenon of monarchy suggested it![2]

At least four notions were implicit in Tylor's evolutionary model. First, there was no longer anything very mysterious about religion; religion's natural origin and subsequent evolutionary development had now been scientifically explained. Second, since monotheism marked the final stage in religion's evolution, religion had now reached the end of a dead-end street. Third, further developments in human society were already dictating the next step for people who wanted to stay on the crest of evolution's wave: abandon religion with its now defunct God, gods or spirits.

Was it not more sensible, if one must trust in something, simply to trust in the evolutionary process itself? Anything which could "create" spirits, gods and even a God and then outmode them must be greater than they!

What, then, was the fourth notion implicit in Tylor's theory? It was the one which would make it possible to test the validity of Tylor's thesis by field research. If Tylor was correct, primitive societies would be devoid of monotheistic presuppositions, since class stratification and the later concept of a monarchy had not yet developed to prompt the notion of monotheism.

Drawn by the impressive elegance of Tylor's theory, dozens of notable scholars gave him their initial support. Probably the most detailed documentation of what followed is found in the writings of Fr. Wilhelm Schmidt, an Austrian Catholic priest who was both a professor at Vienna University and the editor of *Anthropos*, a scholarly scientific journal. For example, in his *Origin and Growth of Religion*, Schmidt wrote:

> [Tylor's theory] with its crushing weight of facts, its smooth and unbroken series of stages of development, and the concise, dispassionate style of its exposition, left no room for opposition . . . for the next three decades it remained "the classical theory," . . . almost without any loss of prestige. Even [Herbert] Spencer's ghost-theory, which immediately succeeded it, could not deprive it of pride of place. . . . A notable proof of the extent to which Tylor's theory influenced the world is the fact that it was accepted by a number of prominent students of ethnology and religion almost without alteration. Such unqualified acceptance is to be found in . . . [3]

Schmidt went on to list 39 European and American scholars who endorsed Tylor's theory, naming the various books and articles in which their endorsements could be found. Included in the list was Scotsman Andrew Lang, whom Schmidt describes as "Tylor's favorite pupil."[4] Early in his career Lang championed Tylor's theory in its struggle against Max Muller's competing "Nature-myth" theory. Result: "Muller . . . was forced to compromise."[5]

Occasionally, even in the heyday of evolutionary theories like Tylor's, a few voices at least *tried* to call attention to scattered reports that even very primitive tribes acknowledged the existence of a Creator. But scholars paid little or no attention. Schmidt describes their attitude as follows:

> The doctrine of progressive Evolution mastered the mind of all Europe, . . . all framers of theories concerning fetishes, ghosts, animism, totemism and magic, if they agreed in nothing else, were at one in this, that the figure of the sky-god must be got rid of from

the earliest stages of religion, as being too high and incomprehensible [for savage minds] . . . unless it was preferred to deduce him from Christian influence. The strength of this universal current of thought was so great, and the resulting discredit into which it brought the notion of the great age of the sky-god so complete, that hardly anyone found courage to oppose it and to draw attention to the quite frequent examples of this exalted sky-god appearing among decidedly primitive peoples, where not the least trace of Christian influence was to be found.[6]

With each apparent breakthrough achieved on the basis of an evolutionary framework, some evolutionists became extremely vocal in predicting the eventual, ultimate triumph of evolution over all competing systems, especially theism. Christian clergyman-philosopher E. De Pressense, in his book *A Study of Origins,* wrote of the increasingly strident antitheism gathering momentum in his day:

> I was struck . . . with the increasing vehemence of the attacks made, not only on Christian theism, but on the very foundations of spiritual religion. If we are to believe the men who come forward as the recognized organs of the scientific world, we must conclude that all that has been affirmed by the disciples of the Gospel . . . is but an empty dream. Our aspirations after a higher world are, to use the figure of one of this school, but as dead leaves whirled aloft into the air, which fall back upon the hand that flung them. Everything is to be reduced to energy, ever transmuted, but ever the same.[7]

De Pressense went on to mention:

> The victory so loudly vaunted in the camps of materialism . . . Those who assert that science has pronounced a final verdict on the world of mind and of conscience . . . the promotion of a materialistic fanaticism at least as extravagant as any fanaticism of the theists. Nightly in our cities we hear the Boanerges of

atheism thundering this credo . . . the premature triumph which materialism claims for itself in its popular manuals of science . . . and in high-sounding newspaper articles.[8]

De Pressense then proceeded to bring "this conflict between the thinkers of our age" before his readers. He added, "I have endeavored to be at once impartial and clear in stating the views held by those with whom I differ . . . I have always borne in mind that a man is often much better than his theories."[9]

De Pressense included a philosophical critique of Tylor's theory in his treatise but, like many others who attempted such critiques, he did not succeed in stemming the tide of evolutionary thought on the origin of religion.

Eleven years later, in 1898, it happened.

That "favorite pupil" of Tylor's, Andrew Lang, allowed himself to read a missionary's report, sent home to supporting churches from a distant field. The missionary said that primitive inhabitants of that distant place already acknowledged the existence of a Creator God even before the missionaries arrived! Schmidt describes Lang's reaction:

His impression was that the missionary had made a mistake. But the further his studies took him the more examples of this kind he met with, and at last he came to the conclusion that this fundamental tenet of Tylor's would not hold water. To this conviction he gave public expression in 1898, in his book *The Making of Religion* . . . Apart from this, Lang was unweariedly busy and on the watch for new particulars to discover and publish, mistakes and misunderstandings to clear up, attacks to repel . . .

Seeing then that [Lang's objections] found lively expression in leading British periodicals, which of course are known everywhere abroad also, and that they represented the new views of a scholar of such wide repute . . . it is hard to understand why the majority of specialists . . . outside Great Britain received Lang's utterances with the deepest silence. . . . This whole attitude of silent rejection was all the more remarkable because the theory of magic, which appeared simultaneously, was everywhere accorded ready discussion and, in a short time, wide acceptance; yet according to . . . its first three supporters . . . Marett, Hubert . . . and Preuss . . . it rested on insecure and merely provisional foundations.[10]

Schmidt comments repeatedly throughout his work on the persistent tendency of scholars to ignore or discredit the sky-god phenomenon. Not until as late as 1922, he says, did the first scientific monograph on the subject appear.[11] It seemed that the possibility of using *any* other aspect of religion as the starting point for the development of religion had to be exhausted before the Sky-God could be considered.

In Schmidt's eyes at least, evolutionary theories like Tylor's seemed *strange* because of this common denominator of indifference among scholars toward the one line of research which they apparently felt would not support an evolutionary explanation.

Virtually ostracized by his fellow scholars in Britain and ignored by scholars in mainland Europe, Andrew Lang wrote: "Like other martyrs of science, I must expect to be thought importunate, tedious, a fellow of one idea and that idea wrong. To resent this would show great want of humor, and a plentiful lack of knowledge of human nature."[12]

Still Lang pressed his attack, relying especially on "the startling discoveries of A. W. Howitt concerning the Supreme Being of the South-East Australian tribes . . . and on information given by Mrs. Langloh Parker concerning [other Australian tribes]. . . . He also made use . . . of facts from the Bushmen, Hottentots, Zulu, Yao, the West African peoples, the Tierra del Fuegians, and somewhat more extensively from the North American Indians."[13]

Long before Lang called public attention to Howitt's Australian research, Tylor himself had read Howitt's papers shortly after they were first published in 1884. What was his response? Schmidt reports: "His only resource . . . was to . . . question the native origin of these gods, referring them to European, and specifically to missionary influence."[14]

Tylor made this reply official six years later in an article entitled "The Limits of Savage Religion." But Howitt, who still did not perceive that his research was undermining Tylor's theory, which he admired, and who later actually criticized Lang for using his research to attack Tylor's theory, had already indicated to Tylor that no such "out" was available.[15]

Other scholars similarly proved that missionary influence could not explain the same phenomenon already showing up in many other parts of the world besides Australia. It was the beginning of the end for Tylor's theory. Schmidt comments that, toward the end, "Tylor . . . could not be induced to speak, despite Lang's direct challenges to [him]."[16]

It was Wilhelm Schmidt himself who, appalled by the lack of recognition given to Lang, threw himself into one of the most extensive research projects ever undertaken by one man. Schmidt began documenting and compiling evidence for "native monotheism," evidence which was now beginning to flow in like a tide from all parts of the world. In 1912 (the year of Lang's death), Schmidt published his mammoth *Ursprung Der Gottesidee* (*The Origin of the Concept of God*). Still more data kept pouring in, so he published another volume, and another, and another until, by 1955, he had accumulated more than 4,000 pages of evidence in a total of 12 large volumes!

The entire thirteenth chapter of Schmidt's *The Origin and Growth of Religion* is devoted to quotations from dozens of anthropologists, showing that acceptance of Schmidt's research was virtually universal. The tide had turned! And yet—

Before its downfall, Tylor's theory had inspired certain scholars to apply his ideas in other fields. One would think that refuting the "mother theory" would cause its "conceptual offspring" in other fields to decline as well. This has not been the case. Some of the conceptual offspring of Tylor's theory took on a life of their own, so to speak, and managed to distance themselves from their mother. Thus when she was axed, they were spared and persist, however unjustifiably, *to this very day*!

Once again, we are indebted to Wilhelm Schmidt for pointing out one such insidious connection: the connection between Tylor's theory and liberal theology.

TYLOR'S THEORY AND LIBERAL THEOLOGY

Schmidt wrote: "A further important conquest for the animistic theory was the field of Old Testament theology. Here the agent was J. Lippert who . . . declared the theory to hold good for the development of the Jewish people and [their] religion. This application of the theory was immediately accepted by two leading theologians of Liberal Protestantism: B. Stade . . . and F. Schwall. . . . They were joined by a long array of other authors, such as R. Smend, J. Benzinger, J. Wellhausen, A. Berthold and others, who sought support for their ideas, not only in the results of textual criticism, which they employed, but in these data provided by ethnological research, as transmitted to them by Tylor's theory."[17]

Schmidt later quotes a Professor Brockelmann as claiming that "Wellhausen . . . was more or less consciously under the influence of . . . E.B. Tylor . . . [and] . . . upposed animism to be the only source of religious life."[18]

It was this Wellhausen who became prominent in developing a famous theory claiming that vestiges of the polytheism which, as required by Tylor's theory, must have preceded the development of biblical monotheism, can still be found in the Old Testament. He claimed that monotheistic priests later tried to expunge earlier statements consistent with polytheism from the Pentateuch, but they overlooked some! The resulting school of Higher Criticism not only weakened the faith of millions of Christians and undermined the vitality of hundreds of thousands of churches worldwide, but also deflected great numbers of unbelievers from taking the Bible seriously. Yet to my knowledge no liberal scholar has ever blown a whistle and said, "Wait! Since we no longer endorse Tylor's theory, why are we still endorsing this orphaned offspring of Tylor's theory?"

Even conservative theologians have often accorded Wellhausen's liberal theology an undeserved compliment by attacking it as if it were a conceptually independent structure. Their attacks might have been more effective had they publicly exposed the fact that Wellhausen's theology is based upon an anthropological theory which most anthropologists no longer endorse.

EVOLUTIONARY THEORY
AND NAZI RACISM

Nineteenth-century theories of biological and cultural evolution strongly implied the probability that one branch of mankind, the European branch, had already outdistanced the rest of mankind in physical and cultural evolution. A writer who dared to develop this implication to its logical conclusions was German philosopher Friedrich Nietzsche (1844-1900).

The views of Nietzsche and of many evolutionists of his time can be illustrated as follows. Picture all human societies as runners in a gigantic cultural "marathon." The goal is to race from the cultural simplicity of the stone age toward the ultimate cultural achievement of an ideal society enjoying technological mastery over nature. It follows that if all the runners begin at the same starting line at the same time and run over the same course toward the same finish line, their participation in the "marathon" will make it possible to judge their respective strengths and weaknesses on one scale. And if the societies of any one genetic branch of mankind tend to "lead the pack," so to speak, it will prove that that branch of mankind has achieved a superior physical evolution as well.

The inevitable conclusion was that European man's highly technological societies were the "lead runners"—those averaging five minutes per mile or better. Other societies were like runners averaging six, seven or eight minutes per mile. Primitive tribes were the slowest of all; they were like marathoners averaging only nine, ten or eleven minutes per mile.

Nietzsche in particular focused attention upon the lead runner in the marathon. Nietzsche named him the "Superman." "Superman" was an individual qualified—because of his more rapid evolutionary development—to dominate mankind. He must achieve that domination by sheer "will to power." Moral qualities were not required, for the superman was, as Nietzsche put it, "beyond good and evil."

No doubt Nietzsche and his fellow evolutionists never dreamed that another German, Franz Boas, would shortly undermine the concept of European racial supremacy. Boas's *The Mind of Primitive Man* (1911) in effect initiated a revision of our illustration of all human societies participating in a single marathon. Boas, in effect, insisted that many "marathons" were being run simultaneously. Each society or group of societies had its own starting line, its own starting time, its own course and its own finish line. Hence it was simply not possible to measure the respective "strengths" and "weaknesses" of societies on one scale! A culture pursuing harmony with nature, for example, should not be judged by the norms of a culture pursuing technological mastery over nature!

That being true, it was simply not valid to use culture as a basis for drawing conclusions about the innate superiority of one genetic branch of mankind over others!

One might have hoped that Boas's refutation of European racism would have spared us from any ill effects potential in racist thinking. But such ideas were not to be expunged so easily. Some three decades after Nietzsche's death, an ambitious German named Adolf Hitler decided that if Europeans were the most highly evolved branch of mankind, he and his fellow Germans were easily the most highly evolved branch of the Europeans, i.e., "the super race."

Hitler accordingly, as head of the super race, wanted to prove himself "the superman." The rest of the story remains one of humanity's worst nightmares.

The point is that another application of nineteenth-century evolutionism managed to survive the shakeup caused by the downfall of Tylor's theory coupled with the general acceptance of Boas's new approach. The result was incalculable suffering for mankind. The mere fact that the originators of a theory may later abandon it does not guarantee that leaders in other fields will automatically abandon it also!

Naturally, Hitler's Nazis did not like Franz Boas or his writings! During the 1930s, they rescinded an honorary doctorate which Kiel University had conferred upon Boas. At the same time, they made public bonfires of Boas's writings in German cities.[19]

Nazi racism, then, was founded upon a deliberate rejection of available evidence.

Tylor's Theory and Communism

Political movements vary drastically in their attitudes toward religion. Some are strongly pro-religious. Others tolerate religion as one of the givens of mankind. Still others exploit religion for political purposes. But Karl Marx, Friedrich Engels and Vladimir Ilich Lenin, the founding fathers of Communism, adopted a rather more ambitious policy. Communism, they determined, must suppress and even, if possible, annihilate religion from the earth!

Communists may find it expedient to exploit religion now and then for specific political reasons, but even then their ultimate aim is still the annihilation of religion.

Annihilating religion, they have often found, requires the annihilation of religious people. Or the forcible removal of children from religious families. Or the use of torture and imprisonment. No matter; as a congenitally anti-religious political system, Communism rampages toward its goal.

Ironically, Communism's anti-religious policy has been an albatross around Communism's neck! Millions of Indonesians, for example, vigorously and decisively foiled a Communist attempt to take control of their homeland in 1965. Their strongest objection to Communist control was the fact that they simply would not tolerate Communist suppression of religion. Apart from that policy, Communism might have won control of Indonesia, a victory that would have helped their cause awesomely!

Why did Communism's founding fathers burden their fledgling political movement with such a grossly disadvantageous policy? Perhaps if Lenin, at least, had foreseen the remarkable ability of religious people to maintain and even disseminate their faith in spite of the worst that Communists could do, he might have entertained second thoughts about making the annihilation of religion a primary goal of Communism.[20]

What persuaded the founding fathers of Communism that annihilating religion was both a feasible and a desirable goal? I have never been satisfied with assumptions that it was simply a personal preference of those involved. The following quote, translated by my friend Hank

Paulson from a German edition of *The Collected Works of Lenin*, shows that Lenin, at least, claimed a rational scientific basis for such a goal:

> Our party program is in its entirety built upon a scientific hence materialistic world view. . . . Our program . . . contains the unveiling of the historical and scientific explanation of the origin of religious mystery. . . . Thus our program necessarily contains the propaganda of atheism.[21]

It is not difficult to discern the influence of Tylor's theory behind such a statement. As Wilhelm Schmidt emphasized repeatedly, Tylor's theory took the minds of scholars in Europe and America by storm in the latter part of the nineteenth century. Lenin, either independently or through Marx or others, must have heard or read that science had at last debunked religion's claim to represent genuine spiritual mysteries. Previously, opponents of religion had relied mainly on philosophical arguments. But wasn't it much more devastating to be able to claim that religion's origin and subsequent development had now been *scientifically* explained—all without the slightest recourse to real spiritual entities?

Further evidence that Tylor's theory influenced Communist attitudes toward religion comes from the fact that Tylor's view of the evolution of religion was taught as the main foundation of atheism in colleges and universities throughout the Communist world. Communist governments, moreover, constantly sent streams of literature as well as teams of lecturers or exchange professors out into the third world and even to western countries to teach Tylor's theory as proven fact! Consider a few instances.

My friend Dr. Wayne Dye of Wycliffe Bible Translators was invited to lecture at a scientific symposium in Papua New Guinea. Also invited were a number of anthropologists from Communist nations. And what did the Communists teach the young Papuan university students in their audience? The validity of Tylor's theory of the origin of religion! It sounded *strange* to Dr. Dye to hear scholars still propagating such concepts in the twentieth century. During breaks, Dye asked the Communist anthropologists how they reconciled their teaching with the fact that theories like Tylor's had been refuted during early decades of this century. To his surprise, they appeared quite unaware that such a refutation had occurred!

Early in 1983, at a student conference convened in San Diego, a freshman from one of Southern California's major universities told me that he was studying undergraduate anthropology under a visiting professor from Communist China. "He has been teaching us Tylor's theory right down the line," the student complained. "Nor has he ever mentioned that the theory has since been abandoned in the light of more recent ethnological research. The entire class, moreover, is lapping it up. I myself would not have known that it was all false had I not read *Eternity in Their Hearts*."

The student's complaint raises an ethical question: Was it just for a university to require students to pay hard-earned tuition so that a Communist could teach them outdated theory subverted as Communist dogma? The students paying for the course trusted the University to hire professors who would teach them *valid* anthropology. The University was betraying that trust. Most likely, the University later had to charge still more tuition so that other professors could help the students unlearn what the Communist professor had taught them.

One cannot blame the Communist professor for teaching the only thing he himself has been taught within the Communist educational system. The fault lies with the University for not screening the professor to ascertain his ability to teach modern anthropology.

A Christian visiting the former socialist Federal Republic of Yugoslavia struck up conversations with various Communists about faith in God. Every Communist responded by defending atheism on the basis of arguments recognizable as Tylor's theory. Some even handed the visitor tracts explaining that it was unscientific to believe in something which, though it claimed to represent spiritual reality, was itself merely a product of evolution. Since the Christian at that time knew nothing of the background of nineteenth-century evolutionary theory, he was unable to score any points against the Communist position.

Clearly, the overthrow of Tylor's theory has not prevented Communists from using it as justification for their ongoing suppression of religion. Marx can hardly be blamed, for he died in 1883—a year before Howitt's papers on native monotheism among Australian Aborigines raised the first major doubts about Tylor's theory. Likewise, Engels died in 1895, three years before Lang published his initially ill-received blockbuster *The Making of Religion*. Perhaps we shall never know the extent to which Lenin may have been exposed to reports of changing opinion in the Western world.

At any rate the problem of "strange" theories about the origin of religion still persists in the modern world. It is easy for scholars living comparatively sheltered lives here in the west to say, "Oh, but we don't hold that position today." It is quite another thing for missionaries scattered across the third world to learn how to counteract the insidious use which hostile political forces still make of such ideas.

My point is not to suggest that someone should have muzzled Tylor! It was fair enough that his ideas should have their "go" in court. Nor is it in any way my purpose to suggest that the science of anthropology per se is untrustworthy. I believe that Christians should seek involvement in anthropology and other social sciences in order to bring the balance of a theistic value system to bear upon such sciences.

If Wilhelm Schmidt had not devoted himself to such an involvement, recognition of the unscientific basis of Tylor's theory might have been delayed for years!

Perhaps one criticism can be made of the liberal scholars who initially opposed or ignored Andrew Lang's objections to Tylor: They accepted Tylor's theory very quickly, not only because of its elegance, but also because it fitted their presuppositions about evolution and the supposed supremacy of European man. They accepted Lang's and Schmidt's opposing evidence with heel-dragging reticence because *their* evidence did not confirm such presuppositions. Had the general response to Lang and Schmidt been as rousing as the earlier response to Tylor, possibly, just possibly, the resulting discussions would have caught Lenin's ear before he began pulling the Iron Curtain down around Russia following the Communist Revolution in 1917 (which was also, incidentally, the year of Tylor's death).

Lenin, if I may give him the benefit of a doubt, might then at least have had second thoughts about resting so many Communist hopes upon Tylor's theory. Communism's anti-religious stance accordingly might have become less rigid.

The fall of the Berlin Wall on November 9, 1989, effectively signaled the end of the Communist rule in Eastern Europe. Shortly thereafter, Poland, East Germany, Czechoslovakia, Bulgaria, Romania and Hungary all abandoned Communist rule. The Iron Curtain had come crashing down in Europe, but Communist ideals still flourish in the Far East. Today, religious freedom continues to be suppressed in Communist nations such as China, Laos, North Korea, Vietnam and, to a lesser extent, Cuba (in 1998, Pope John Paul II was allowed to visit the country—the first time such permission has been granted since the Cuban Communist Revolution of 1959).

Hopefully, this review of the history of the matter will enable Christians to be not only better informed but also better able to respond to some of the forces opposed to the gospel in the world today. It might also give great encouragement to Christians who are still under Communist oppression in these countries to hear that even science has officially rejected the basis Communism uses to discredit religious faith.

Before leaving the subject of "Scholars with Strange Theories," I want to comment on the controversy surrounding anthropologist Margaret Mead's first book, *Coming of Age in Samoa*. Although this debate isn't getting the buzz that it once did several decades ago, students of anthropology will no doubt be familiar with Mead's research and her views on the relationship between culture and developmental stages in young adults. Mead's first book, according to some, has had about as liberalizing an influence on the way we raise and educate our young as has Dr. Spock's famous book on child rearing.

In 1983, an Australian anthropologist named Derek Freeman strongly criticized Mead (who died in 1978) in his book *Margaret Mead and Samoa: The Making and Unmaking of an Anthropological Myth* for giving the public misinformation about Samoan culture. Freeman stated that the whole matter would not be a critical issue at all had not liberals like George Bernard Shaw, Havelock Ellis and many others decided to lend Mead's book a visibility and influence out of all proportion to its worth. That is not to discredit Margaret Mead's life work as a whole.

Conservatives should bear in mind that the controversy in debates such as these is not between liberals and conservatives, but rather between two groups of liberals, neither of which especially wants the outcome to favor conservative causes.

PART II

The Gospel Prepared for the World

—The Abraham Factor—

CHAPTER 5

The 4,000-Year Connection

Dr. Ralph Winter, director of the United States Center for World Mission in Pasadena, California, sometimes likes to startle audiences by saying things they think can't possibly be true—but are! For example: "Most Christians think," Dr. Winter once exclaimed, "that the Bible doesn't really emphasize missions. They see it as a sort of afterthought Christ had at the very end of His ministry—as if He snapped His fingers at the last minute before His ascension into heaven and said, 'Oh, by the way, men, there's just one more thing . . .'

"And then, cold turkey, He rocked them back on their heels with this unprecedented, virtually unforeshadowed command about taking the gospel out into all the world.

"But as a matter of fact," Dr. Winter continued, "the Bible actually *begins* with missions, maintains missions as its central theme throughout, and then climaxes in the Apocalypse with spontaneous outbursts of joy because the missionary mandate has been fulfilled!"

Dr. Winter paused to rearrange his notes, while in the audience before him one eyebrow after another furrowed with a question. Then someone raised a hand and voiced the question which was on everyone's mind: "Dr. Winter, the Bible begins with a statement that God created the heavens and the earth. How can you find missions in that?"

Just what the scholarly doctor was waiting for!

"The main theme of the Bible," he responded, his eyes twinkling over the rims of his glasses, "is God blessing all peoples on Earth with a blessing first given to Abraham. And where does God promise to bless all peoples on Earth through Abraham?"

"In Genesis chapter 12," someone replied.

"Genesis chapter 12, then, is the real beginning of the Bible," Dr. Winter continued. "Everything prior to Genesis 12 is the introduction. Equally inspired, yes! But the introduction nonetheless. The main theme doesn't get underway until Genesis 12. Let's look at it."

Curiously, I leafed through Genesis to the twelfth chapter and read the first three verses. I had read them many times before. Now I realized that I had underestimated their significance. Those three verses contain Yahweh's initial articulation of something Jews and Christians together call the *Abrahamic Covenant*. Authors of other parts of the Bible sometimes call that covenant "the promises" because several such are included in it. Other times they call it "the promise," in the singular, because the various promises included in the covenant together constitute *one* coherent purpose of God.

I saw that the various promises contained in the covenant can be arranged under two main headings. I call them *the top line* and *the bottom line*. Let's look at *the top line* first: "I will make you into a great nation," Yahweh began, "and I will bless you; I will make your name great, and you will be a blessing. I will bless those who bless you, and whoever curses you I will curse!"

So-called higher critics have snidely suggested that the Abrahamic Covenant was really just another example of a petty tribal god whetting the selfishness of an exclusive little clique of followers with promises of exclusive blessing. That is because they are so high above the text in their intellectual pride that they cannot see what it is really saying. Note that in the very midst of this flurry of promises regarding the political, personal and social enrichment of Abraham, a qualifying phrase occurs: ". . . and you will be a blessing."

And that phrase presages the bottom line: ". . . AND ALL PEO-PLES ON EARTH WILL BE BLESSED THROUGH YOU."

These words bring a hush upon thoughtful readers. We sense immediately that the God who would speak such words is no petty tribal god. He is a God whose plans are both benign and universal, spanning all ages and cultures. If He retaliates against enemies of Abraham, it is not just to protect Abraham, but also to keep the enemies from extinguishing a fire kindled to warm the whole world!

Clearly the Abrahamic Covenant did not mark the first time God revealed Himself to men. Adam, Cain, Abel, Seth, Enoch, Noah, Job and no doubt many others right on through to Abraham's contemporary, Melchizedek, had received direct communication from God. God even revealed Himself through a dream to Abimelech, a Philistine king (see Gen. 20:6). All of these prior revelations center around (1) the fact of God's existence; (2) creation; (3) the rebellion and fall of man; (4) the need for a sacrifice to appease God and the crafty attempts of devils to make men sacrifice to them; (5) the great Flood; (6) the sudden appearance of many languages and the resulting dispersion of mankind into many peoples; and finally (7) an acknowledgment of man's need of some further revelation that will seal man back into a blessed relationship with God.

These seven major facts which were known before Abraham's time are still included—in a declining order of statistical occurrence—among the main components of folk religions worldwide. The degree to which any folk religion has maintained its hold on truth can be measured by how many of these seven components it still retains and with what clarity. On this basis, the Karen folk religion discovered by Boardman, Wade, Mason and others in Burma was perhaps the "purest" folk religion left on Earth in modern times.

These surviving elements found throughout the world comprise what is sometimes called *general revelation*. Since Melchizedek was the main representative of that kind of revelation in Abraham's day, I have identified that kind of revelation as the *Melchizedek Factor* in history.

The Abrahamic Covenant, however, rises like an island in the midst of the sea of general revelation. That island is called *special revelation*. It is the *Abraham Factor* in history. We have already learned something about the Melchizedek factor in earlier chapters. Now we must study the Abraham factor.

How does the Abraham factor of special revelation differ from the preceding general revelation? First, special revelation is always associated with an inspired canonical record. Moses apparently compiled earlier records to write Genesis—the beginning of that canon. Then he added Exodus, Leviticus, Numbers and Deuteronomy. Apart from special revelation's unique emphasis upon preserving a written record, mankind would have been left without any authoritative account of the wellspring from which general revelation later spread across the earth.

The writer of the New Testament Epistle to the Hebrews calls specific attention to the fact that general revelation, by Melchizedek's time, was already detached from a traceable historical tie-in with special revelation. He points out the unusual fact that Moses, although carefully recording the lineage of every other major person in the patriarchal age, does not record the names of Melchizedek's parents, nor the historical context of his birth, nor his age at death (see Heb. 7:3). He does not say, "Melchizedek, son of . . ." He emphasizes also that Melchizedek's priesthood—unlike the later Levitical priesthood which came through Abraham—was not based upon physical membership in a priestly lineage. A priest of this Melchizedekian type was always "just there," so to speak. You could never predict where you might find (or not find) one of them!

This has always been a characteristic of general revelation—it's *just-thereness*! The writer of the Epistle to the Hebrews emphasizes also that the Messiah who came among men in fulfillment of every spiritual reality foreshadowed by the Levitical priestly system was also at the same time "a priest forever, in the order of Melchizedek" (Ps. 110:4; see also Heb. 5:4-10; 6:20; 7:15-22). Christ, in other words, is Lord of *both* general and special revelation.

The unity of both general and special revelation under Christ is indicated also by the apostle John, who wrote: "The true light [Christ] that gives light to every man [through general revelation]" was coming into the world (i.e., to shine upon men in a new and special way. John states also: "The light shines in the darkness [the Sodom factor], but the darkness has not overpowered it" (John 1:5, alternate rendering; see footnote in *NIV*).

Scientists have discovered recently that even physical light occurs in two forms—*ambient* and *coherent*. Ambient light, such as daylight, lamplight, firelight and so on, occurs naturally whenever certain factors prevail. Coherent light, however, occurs only in a laser, and therefore requires special, deliberate preparation and design. In ambient light, individual photons are scattered indiscriminately, like strollers meandering through a park. In coherent light, individual photons are organized into a "solid" beam, as if the "strollers" suddenly become organized and march lockstep through the park like an army! And coherent light can accomplish wonders beyond the scope of ambient light. It can, for example, eat through metal, or even excise cataracts from the eyes of the blind!

Thus general revelation could perhaps be called *ambient* revelation, and special revelation, in this parallelism, becomes *coherent* revelation, for it is systematized to bring, not merely illumination, but "blessing"!

Tracing the emergence of special revelation through the Abrahamic Covenant, the promised "blessing" turns out to be redemption through the Messiah. And the target of that blessing is "all peoples on earth." Not *every person* on Earth—otherwise the Abrahamic Covenant would be a basis for a doctrine of universal salvation!

The phrase "all peoples" constitutes a divine recognition of ethnic distinctions within our race. The same God who caused the proliferation of human cultures by His sovereign intervention at Babel now targets His special blessing through Abraham toward every "people" thus formed. In fact, Moses mentions 36 pagan peoples by name in the course of describing Yahweh's dealings with Abraham.

Furthermore, God is so determined to fulfill His promise to bless Abraham and make him a blessing to all peoples that He actually *binds Himself by an oath* to emphasize His determination (see Gen. 22:15-18).

And the oath covers both the top and bottom lines of the covenant (see specifically Gen. 22:18).

This oath taking—a very serious matter from the viewpoint of Semitic peoples—triggers extensive commentary again from the author of the Epistle to the Hebrews. He states that God thus staked His infinite reputation upon the fulfillment of the covenant so that all may know that it represents "the *unchanging nature of his purpose*" (Heb. 6:17, emphasis added).

What, then, is that purpose? To guarantee that both the top and bottom lines of the Abrahamic Covenant come true! To bless Abraham and his seed (which, as we shall soon see, includes more than just the *Jewish* race), and then to make Abraham's seed a blessing to all peoples.

Now—let's ask the inevitable question: Do the Scriptures from Genesis 12 onward show Yahweh pursuing the fulfillment of His oath-bound promises to Abraham—including the bottom line? Or does Scripture indicate that Yahweh, having bound Himself by that solemn oath, sort of drifted off course and got sidetracked into pursuing other goals? First of all—have you ever noticed that so much of the Old Testament is dedicated to narratives of various sons and daughters of Abraham being a blessing to non-Jewish peoples?

Just in case you haven't noticed this special significance of your favorite Old Testament dramas, let me point out that, for example:

1. Abraham himself bore witness to *Canaanites, Philistines, Hittites* and, rather negatively, to *Egyptians*.
2. Joseph was a son of Abraham who made up for his forefather's lack of a clear witness to the *Egyptian nation*! Joseph blessed Egyptians in truly amazing ways.
3. The spies who entered Jericho before it was destroyed became a blessing to Rahab, a *Canaanite* harlot, and her family.
4. Naomi, a daughter of Abraham, was a blessing to two *Moabite* women, Ruth and Orpah.
5. Moses became a blessing to Jethro, his *Midianite* father-in-law.
6. King David caused even his enemies, the *Philistines*, to acknowledge God's greatness.

7. The prophet Elijah was a blessing to a *Sidonian* widow in Zarephath.
8. The prophet Elisha, likewise, was a blessing to Naaman, a *Syrian*.
9. Jonah, however reluctantly, became a blessing to the Gentile population of *Nineveh*.
10. King Solomon was a blessing to the *Sabaean* "Queen of the South."
11. Daniel and his three colleagues, Shadrach, Meshach and Abednego, were a blessing to *Babylonians*.
12. Esther and her uncle Mordecai were a blessing to the entire *Persian Empire*.
13. Ezekiel, Jeremiah, Ezra, Nehemiah and other prophets declared the Word of the Lord to various *Gentile* nations.

Clearly, the Holy Spirit has employed a principle of selectivity in deciding which biographical narratives should or should not find inclusion in the Old Testament canon. Out of tens of thousands of other worthy narratives that doubtless could have been included, He has favored *narratives which illustrate both the top and bottom lines of the Abrahamic Covenant at work in the lives of sons and daughters of Abraham.*

Not only so, but there are also more than 300 *declarative* passages in the Old Testament which amplify God's oath-sealed promise to bless all nations on Earth (see, for example, Ps. 67 and Isa. 49:6).

Moving forward now to the New Testament, do we find God still adhering to His ancient commitment to both the top and bottom lines, or drifting from it?

The apostle Paul, for one, leaves us in no doubt whatever that the New Testament is really a continuation of God's original purpose revealed in the Abrahamic Covenant. For example, five times in just one chapter of one Epistle—Galatians—Paul emphasizes the unbreakable connection between the Abrahamic Covenant and the New Testament gospel:

1. "The Scripture foresaw that God would justify the Gentiles by faith, and announced the gospel in advance to Abraham:

'All nations will be blessed through you'" (Gal. 3:8). Paul saw the New Testament gospel as already having a 2,000-year connection with the Abrahamic Covenant. But there is more.

2. "He redeemed us in order that the blessing given to Abraham [i.e. the "top line" blessing] might come to the Gentiles [fulfilling the "bottom line" promise] through Christ Jesus" (Gal. 3:14). Paul continued:

3. "The promises were spoken to Abraham and to his seed. The Scripture does not say 'and to seeds,' meaning many people, but 'and to your seed,' meaning one person, who is Christ" (Gal. 3:16). In a special singular sense, then, Jesus Christ was *the seed* of Abraham, Paul states this specific identification of Christ as the Seed of Abraham again.

4. Verse 19: "[The law] was added . . . until the Seed to whom the promise referred had come."

5. But there is a more general sense in which all who stand identified with Jesus Christ by their faith in Him are also the "seed" of Abraham: "If you belong to Christ, then you are Abraham's seed, and heirs according to the promise" (Gal. 3:29).

We Christians have generally failed to appreciate the fact that Paul and the other apostles saw the Abrahamic Covenant as basic to everything Christ came to accomplish. That covenant was therefore basic to their own labors and to their writings as well. By means of the Abrahamic Covenant (and especially its "bottom line"), they saw their own lives fitting into God's long-term historical perspective. And they used the bottom line as their main means of explaining to their fellow Jews why it was necessary for them to reach out to Gentile peoples!

Notice, for example, Peter's clear reference to the "bottom line" in Acts 3:25, spoken in the aftermath of Christ's clear command to the apostles to "be witnesses unto him" from Jerusalem to the "ends of the earth." "And you are heirs of the prophets and of the covenant God made with your fathers. He said to Abraham, 'Through your offspring all peoples on earth will be blessed.'"

Peter then explained the point of the "bottom line" by saying: "When God raised up his servant [i.e., when He called Jesus to His ministry as Messiah, as in Acts 3:22], he sent him first to you to bless you [i.e., in fulfillment of 'the top line']" (Acts 3:26). Peter has simply referred to the top and bottom lines in reverse order. Peter's words, "first to you to bless you" imply that God had also a contiguous second purpose to bless Gentiles according to the promise just quoted.

Paul's perception that the "bottom line" foreshadowed the New Testament gospel's "breakout" into the Gentile world was not merely a casual insight. Paul actually calls it a "mystery made known to me by revelation" (Eph. 3:3). He also calls it an "insight . . . not made known to men in other generations as it has now been revealed by the Spirit of God's holy apostles and prophets" (Eph. 3:4-5).

He then defines his profound insight: "This mystery is that through the gospel the Gentiles [i.e., the 'all peoples' of the bottom line] are heirs together with Israel, members together of one body, and sharers together in *the promise* [the Abrahamic Covenant] in Christ Jesus" (Eph. 3:6, emphasis added). Paul says essentially the same thing again in Romans 16:25-26 and in Colossians 1:25-27. Also, in Romans 15:8-9 he writes: "For I tell you that Christ has become a servant of the Jews on behalf of God's truth, *to confirm the promises made to the patriarchs, so that the Gentiles may glorify God for His mercy*" (emphasis added).

Paul then expresses his desire to "make plain to everyone [his] administration of this mystery, which for ages past was kept hidden in God" (Eph. 3:9). This mystery—and Paul's administration of it—is in accord with "[God's] eternal purpose which he accomplished in Christ Jesus our Lord" (Eph. 3:11; see also Rom. 15; 16:25-26).

Paul's words remind us of the statement in the Epistle to the Hebrews concerning "the unchanging nature of his purpose," as indicated by the oath God took over the Abrahamic Covenant.

Why, then, have tens of thousands of Bible teachers and Bible commentators throughout Christendom failed to reflect the centrality of the Abrahamic Covenant with its top and bottom lines in their teaching and lecturing? Followers of Christ around the world and down through the centuries could have had 100 times more missionary vigor if seminary professors, pastors and church school teachers had understood and communicated this central theme as the Bible communicates it.

The Abrahamic Covenant, in all the manifold out-workings of both its top and its bottom lines, is the very backbone of the Bible—the spinal column of special revelation! Teaching which does not acknowledge that spinal column will inevitably have a certain spinelessness about it. It will—quite literally—lack backbone! And it will tend to leave Christians less motivated than they would otherwise be to pass on the blessings they have received, not merely to their own kind of people, but to all peoples on Earth.

We can hardly expect the Church to manifest a Pauline zeal for all remaining unblessed peoples if we ourselves have failed to infuse the Church with the very historical perspectives which accelerated Paul himself to that high level of zeal. To use a parallel, physicists concerned with high energy physics tell us that no atomic particle can be accelerated to high energies unless: (1) it is a charged particle to begin with; (2) it is caught in the grip of a powerful magnetic field; and (3) that particle is moved by the magnetic field in relation to a very long tunnel, the "accelerator."

By analogy, we first have to become "charged particles" through our individual conversion to Jesus Christ. Then we must be caught in the grip of a surrounding magnetic field—the Holy Spirit's power permeating the Body of Christ. That magnetic field must then move us in alignment with a very long tunnel—God's 4,000-year-old purpose in history—a purpose defined by just one thing: the Abrahamic Covenant. That covenant's importance, therefore, cannot be overstated. To perceive oneself in relation to that 4,000-year-old purpose of God is to become a profoundly "charged" person. It is impossible to imagine a stronger stimulation to high motivation in seeking the fulfillment of God's plan for the world.

To imply that God is no longer concerned about fulfilling His two ancient promises to Abraham would be to imply that God's mind has wandered—that it has somehow slipped His mind that He bound Himself by an oath to fulfill those two ancient promises.

Remember the response of the Epistle to the Hebrews: "It is impossible for God to lie [or forget]" (6:18).

This, then, is what I mean by "the 4,000-year connection." To see oneself as an instrument in God's now 4,000-year-old purpose to impart blessing to all peoples is to jettison at once all feelings of insignificance, indecision and purposelessness. That very long historical perspective, by the spiritual magnetic field which permeates it, begins at once to accelerate us toward the greatest destiny any finite being can possibly find.

Just be sure you are a charged particle to begin with—a genuine believer in Jesus Christ. Otherwise that magnetic field and the accelerator will have no effect upon you whatever. They will simply leave you standing where you are.

Hundreds of millions of Christians have listened to hundreds of thousands of preachers deliver hundreds of thousands of sermons based on the great anthems of the Apocalypse, anthems sung by heavenly beings to celebrate the great gathering of the redeemed in heaven. You will find these recorded in the apostle John's Revelation, the final book of the Bible. But precious few of those preachers or their listeners seem to have understood what John was really telling us when he quoted the 24 elders, for example, singing in one of those anthems: "You [Lamb of God] are worthy . . . because you were slain, and with your blood you purchased men for God from *every tribe and language and people and nation*. You have made them to be a kingdom and priests to serve our God, and they will reign on earth" (Rev. 5:9-10, emphasis added).

And when John described his own breathtaking vision of "a great multitude that no one could count, from every nation, tribe, people, and language, standing before the throne and in front of the Lamb" (Rev. 7:9), what was he really communicating to us?

Likewise, when he was told by an angel that he "must prophesy again about many peoples, nations, languages and kings" (Rev. 10:11), what significance do you discern?

And what comes to mind when he in Revelation 11:9 states that "men from every people, tribe, language and nation" will behold the miracle of the two witnesses? And when he states that the beast (Antichrist) will for a season exercise authority over every tribe, people, language and nation (see Rev. 13:7)?

What comes through in his description of another angel who proclaims "the eternal gospel . . . to every nation, tribe, language and people" (Rev. 14:6)?

Surely John is describing not just the consummation of history, but the consummation of God's *special purpose in history* to bless all peoples on Earth through Abraham's Seed—Jesus Christ! John could as easily have described the scenes mentioned with a single Greek noun for the word "mankind." Instead he explores the entire vocabulary of the Greek language, mustering every noun available to denote the kind of ethnic subdivisions of mankind which were the original God-ordained targets of the Abrahamic "blessing."

In other words, John is telling us through such prophecies that God will pursue His ancient purpose to the very end—when He will be free from the obligation He took upon Himself by that ancient oath. For it is the "unchanging nature of His purpose"!

Now for a very suspenseful question. The apostles reveal full awareness of the centrality of the Abrahamic Covenant in their writings—but what about Jesus Christ Himself? Do the four Gospels reveal that He manifested awareness of the covenant as foundational to His ministry? If, after all I have said on this subject, it turns out that our Lord Himself seemed blissfully unaware of any obligation relating to "the bottom line," and therefore did not manifest an all-peoples perspective, the entire point of this book would be undermined.

A Messiah for All Peoples

"Your father Abraham rejoiced at the thought of seeing my day; he saw it and was glad" (John 8:56).

Every time I read that sentence I can almost hear father Abraham's patriarchal laughter echoing through the centuries! But who uttered that sentence? Whose "day" is it that filled father Abraham with anticipation?

The speaker was Jesus of Nazareth, a descendant of Abraham born 1,900 years after Abraham's time. Incredulous Jews, startled by such an awesome claim, objected: "You are not yet fifty years old . . . and you have seen Abraham!" (v. 57).

His second even more daring reply blew the doors off their minds: "I tell you the truth . . . before Abraham was born, I am!" (v. 58).

"I Am" was another Jewish name for God!

Thunderstruck Jews picked up stones to stone Him, but Jesus eluded them (see v. 59). Not many months later, that same Jesus, "carrying his own cross . . . went out to The Place of the Skull (which in Aramaic is called Golgotha). Here they crucified him" (John 19:17-18).

Where was Golgotha—The Place of the Skull—located? Just outside the wall of Jerusalem and within, at the most, 1,600 meters of the tip of Mount Moriah. King Solomon, centuries earlier, had erected the first Jewish Temple on Mount Moriah, probably to commemorate the exact spot where Abraham stretched Isaac upon that pile of wood (see Gen. 22:1-19). It was there that Yahweh placed Himself under oath to fulfill both lines of the Abrahamic Covenant.

Note, however, that the Genesis record does not say that Abraham offered Isaac on Mount Moriah, but rather in "the region of Moriah." Clearly, if Abraham had stood on the very peak of Moriah (more pronounced in those days than it is now), it would have been easier to describe the location as such. Smaller spurs or ridges below the main peak would not have been as easy to name. But if the event had occurred much more than 1,600 meters away from Mount Moriah, it would more readily have been associated with other nearby hills, some of which were more prominent than Moriah.

It is possible, therefore, that Golgotha could have been the very site of Isaac's ordeal. If indeed Yahweh intended that Jesus' agony also should occur on that very site, it was essential that He leave Jewish historians with an inexact record of its location, otherwise commemorative shrines would surely have been built there, making it impossible for Roman soldiers to use the site for Jesus' crucifixion.

In any case, a descendant of Abraham named Jesus—though innocent of any crime—was slain while fastened upon wood which He Himself carried to His execution site. Isaac, also having no crime charged against him, carried wood to his execution site and then was laid upon the wood. He was spared only by the intervention of God. And the site in both cases was approximately, if not exactly, the same.

Many other parallels between Isaac and Jesus could be cited, but most important of all—Jesus' entire life, death and resurrection were inextricably linked with Yahweh's age-old promise to share the "blessings of Abraham" with all peoples on Earth.

As if to emphasize this fact, Matthew, a chronicler of Jesus' life begins his account by tracing the Lord's ancestry back across 42 unbroken generations to none other than Abraham himself! Jesus' physical lineage, however, was merely foundational. Millions of Jews throughout history could trace ancestry to Abraham. Jesus' own mother, Mary, proclaimed in her famous song of praise that Yahweh, through Jesus' advent, was bringing forth far more than just another physical descendant of Abraham. That advent was a sign that Yahweh, in Mary's words, was "remembering to be merciful to Abraham and his descendants forever, even as he said to our fathers" (Luke 1:54-55).

Also Jesus' Uncle Zechariah cited his nephew's coming as proof that Yahweh had remembered "his holy covenant, the oath he swore to our father Abraham." Then Zechariah heightened anticipation still further when he likened Jesus' advent to a "rising sun . . . come to us from heaven to shine *on those living in darkness and in the shadow of death*" (Luke 1:72-73,78-79, emphasis added).

References to people "living in darkness" and in "the shadow of death" were commonly understood by Jews as designating Gentiles (see Matt. 4:15-16). We are getting closer to that bottom line of the Abrahamic promise! Finally . . .

Aged Simeon, a devout Jew who met Joseph, Mary and baby Jesus in the Temple at Jerusalem, articulated ever so eloquently that wider purpose of Messiah's coming, declaring before Yahweh: "My eyes have seen your salvation, which you have prepared *in the sight of all people, a light for revelation to the Gentiles* and for glory to your people Israel" (Luke 2:30-32, emphasis added).

Likewise Jesus' forerunner, John the Baptist, constantly quoted Isaiah 40:3-5 as justification for his ministry of preparing "the way for the Lord" by making "straight paths for him." For what purpose? That *"all mankind will see God's salvation"* (Luke 3:4,6, emphasis added).

The implication of John's words stung some Jews; they, God's chosen people, were guilty of making their ways "crooked," thus preventing the rest of mankind from "seeing God's salvation," as God's promise to Abraham required.

Some Jews apparently bristled with resentment, suggesting it was not proper to bring such accusations against "children of Abraham."

But John's response to their using Abraham as an excuse for indolence was swift and sharp. "Do not begin to say to yourselves, 'We have Abraham as our father.' For I tell you that out of these stones God can raise up children for Abraham. The ax is already at the root of the trees, and every tree [including those called 'Abrahamic'] that does not produce good fruit will be cut down and thrown into the fire" (Luke 3:8-9).

With these words John the Baptist foreshadowed the new thing Yahweh was about to do through Jesus—call a new kind of Abrahamic offspring out of rough "stonepiles" of the Gentile world. Those thus called would become "living stones" in God's spiritual temple. And this time God's basis for selection would not be mere physical descendancy, but repentance and faith providentially engendered.

"A light for revelation to the Gentiles!" A "Sun" to rise upon people "living in darkness and in the shadow of death!" A bringer of "salvation . . . prepared in the sight of all people!" All the pointers were unmistakable: Jesus was destined to be not merely a man for all seasons as the Jewish Messiah, but also a man for all peoples—the Light of even the Gentile world!

How fitting then, that Jesus, the Jewish Messiah, should have some Gentile blood in Him.

Besides Jesus' mother, Mary, only four women are mentioned in the male-dominated genealogies of Matthew 1 and Luke 3. And all four are Gentile women who share in Messiah's lineage. Tamar, Judah's wife, came out of a Canaanite background (see Gen. 38). Rahab, the harlot of Jericho who gave shelter to Hebrew spies just before the famous fall of that ancient city, married a Hebrew named Salmon, and with him shares the lineage of Jesus Christ (see Matt. 1:5). Likewise Ruth, a woman of a despised Gentile region called Moab, married Salmon and Rahab's son, Boaz; gave birth to a son, Obed; and thus also became a "mother" of Jesus (see v. 5). Finally, Bathsheba, whom King David married, is thought to have come from among the Hittites (see 2 Sam. 11:3).

How fitting also that God should use a decree of a Gentile emperor, Caesar Augustus, to guarantee that Jesus would come to birth in Bethlehem, the city of David, fulfilling a prophecy of an Old Testament prophet named Micah (see Mic. 5:2). How fitting again that apparently non-Jewish scholar-magicians from the Middle East were among the first to celebrate Jesus' birth (see Matt. 2:1). And that Jesus found refuge from the wrath of Herod, a merciless Jewish king, in Gentile Egypt (see Matt. 2:14)!

Finally, how appropriate that Jesus began His public ministry in a sector of Galilee bordered by Gentile Syria on the north and Gentile Decapolis on the east! Actually, Galilee bordered disreputable Samaria with its half-breed population as well! Galilean ground was definitely not considered prime real estate! Yet Jesus honored that region with His first public sermons!

Matthew, one of Jesus' disciples, recorded this fact as a fulfillment of the prophet Isaiah's comment about "Galilee of the Gentiles": "The people living in darkness have seen a great light: on those living in the land of the shadow of death a light has dawned" (Matt. 4:15-16; see also Isa. 9:1-2).

"Large crowds from Galilee, the Decapolis, Jerusalem, Judea and the region across the Jordan followed" Him, Matthew comments (4:25). "News about him spread all over Syria, and people brought to him all who were ill . . . and he healed them" (v. 24).

The die was cast! In spite of heavy pressure and criticism (including some from His own disciples), Jesus was to keep His ministry true to the open character thus established at the beginning. A man for all peoples, His eyes, ears, hands and heart would always be as attentive to Gentiles and Samaritans as to Jews, His own kinsmen. And He expected His disciples to learn from His example!

Millions of Christians know, of course, that Jesus, at the end of His ministry, commanded His disciples to "go and make disciples of all [peoples]" (Matt. 28:19). We respectfully honor this last and most incredible command He gave with an august title—the Great Commission. And yet millions of us deep down in our hearts secretly believe, if our deeds are an accurate barometer of our beliefs (and Scripture says they are), that Jesus really uttered that awesome command without giving His disciples ample warning.

Read cursorily through the four Gospels and the Great Commission looks like a sort of afterthought paper-clipped onto the end of the main body of Jesus' teachings. As Dr. Winter pointed out, it is almost as if our

Lord, after divulging everything that was really close to His heart, snapped His fingers and said, "Oh, yes, by the way, men, there's one more thing. I want you all to proclaim this message to everyone in the world, regardless of his language and culture. That is, of course, if you have the time and feel disposed."

Did Jesus hit His disciples with the Great Commission cold turkey? Did He just spring it on them at the last minute without fair warning and then slip away to heaven before they had a chance to interact with Him about its feasibility? Did He fail to provide reasonable demonstration on ways to fulfill it?

How often we Christians read the four Gospels without discerning the abundant evidence God has provided for an entirely opposite conclusion! Consider, for example, how compassionately Jesus exploited the following encounters with Gentiles and Samaritans to help His disciples think in cross-cultural terms.

On one occasion (see Matt. 8:5-13), a Roman centurion, a Gentile, approached Jesus with a request on behalf of his paralyzed servant. Jews, on this occasion, urged Jesus to comply. "This man deserves to have you do this, because he loves our nation and has built our synagogue," they explained.

In fact, walls and pillars of a synagogue built probably by that very centurion still stand 2,000 years later near the north shore of the Sea of Galilee! But notice the implication of the Jews' reasoning. They were saying, in effect, that if the centurion had not thus helped them, neither should Jesus help the centurion or his pitifully paralyzed servant! How clannish of them! Little wonder Jesus could not help sighing occasionally, "O unbelieving and perverse generation . . . how long shall I stay with you? How long shall I put up with you?" (Matt. 17:17).

Jesus responded to the centurion, "I will go and heal him." At that moment the centurion said something quite unexpected: "Lord, I do not deserve to have you come under my roof. But just say the word, and my servant will be healed. For I myself am a man under authority, with soldiers under me. . . . When Jesus heard this, he was astonished," wrote Matthew. What was so astonishing? Simply this—the centurion's military experience had taught him something about authority. As water always flows downhill, so also authority always flows down an echelon (a chain of command). Whoever submits to authority from a higher level of an echelon is privileged also to wield authority over lower levels. Jesus, the centurion noticed, walked in perfect submission to God; therefore, Jesus must have perfect authority over everything below Him on the greatest echelon of all—the cosmos! Ergo! Jesus must possess infallible ability to command the nerves and muscles of the sick servant's body to return to a state of health!

"I tell you the truth," Jesus exclaimed, "I have not found anyone in Israel with such great faith!" As in many other discourses, Jesus exploited the occasion to teach His disciples that Gentiles have just as great a potential for faith as Jews! And they make just as valid objects for the grace of God too!

Determined to maximize the point, Jesus went on to say: "I say to you that many will come from the east and the west [Luke, a Gentile writer, adds in his parallel account: 'and from the north and the south'], and will take their places at the feast with Abraham, Isaac and Jacob in the kingdom of heaven. But the subjects of the kingdom [this could only mean the Jews as God's chosen people] will be thrown outside, into the darkness, where there will be weeping and gnashing of teeth" (Matt. 8:7-12; Luke 7:9; 13:28-29).

What would you guess that Abraham, Isaac and Jacob will be celebrating with that host of *Gentile* guests? The fulfillment of Yahweh's "bottom-line" promise to bless all peoples, of course!

Intimations of the Great Commission to follow could hardly have been clearer! Wait, there is much more!

Still later, a Canaanite woman from the region of Tyre and Sidon begged Jesus' mercy on behalf of her demon-possessed daughter. Jesus at first feigned indifference. His disciples, glad no doubt to see their Messiah turn a cold shoulder to a bothersome Gentile, concurred at once with what they thought were His true feelings. "Send her away," they argued, "for she keeps crying out after us" (see Matt. 15:21-28).

Little did they know that Jesus was setting them up. "I was sent only to the lost sheep of Israel," He said to the woman. Having already manifested an apparent insensitivity toward the woman, Jesus now manifests an apparent inconsistency also. He has already healed many Gentiles. On what basis does He now reject this one's plea? One can imagine the disciples nodding grimly. Still they did not suspect. Undissuaded, the Canaanite woman actually knelt at Jesus' feet, pleading, "Lord, help me!"

"It is not right to take the children's bread"—metaphor for God's blessings upon Jews in accord with the "top line." Then He added the crusher—"and toss it to their dogs!" "Dogs" was a standard epithet Jews reserved for Gentiles, especially Gentiles who tried to intrude upon Jewish religious privacy and privilege. In other words, Jesus now complements His earlier "insensitivity" and "inconsistency" with even worse "cruelty." Notice also that Jesus' words stand in direct contradiction to the "bottom line" of the Abrahamic Covenant.

Was this really the Savior of the world talking? No doubt His disciples thought His reference quite appropriate for the occasion. But just when their chests were swollen to the full with pride of race, the Canaanite woman must have caught a twinkle in Jesus' eye and realized the truth!

"Yes, Lord," she replied ever so humbly, not to mention subtly, "but even the dogs eat the crumbs that fall from their master's table!" (Matt. 15:21-27; see also Mark 7:26-30).

"Woman, you have great faith!" Jesus glowed. "Your request is granted!" No, He was not being fickle! This was what He intended to do all along. Immediately preceding this event, Jesus had taught His disciples about the difference between *real* versus *figurative* uncleanness. This was His way of driving the point home.

"And her daughter was healed from that very hour," Matthew records (v. 28).

When on a later occasion Jesus and His band approached a certain Samaritan village, the Samaritans refused to welcome Him. James and John, two disciples whom Jesus nicknamed "sons of thunder" for their fiery tempers, were incensed. "Lord," they exclaimed indignantly (stamping their feet?), "do you want us to call fire down from heaven and destroy them?"

Jesus turned and rebuked James and John. Some ancient manuscripts add that He said, "You do not know what kind of spirit you are of, for the Son of Man did not come to destroy men's lives, but to save them" (Luke 9:51-55, including a footnote).

With those words, Jesus identified Himself as a Savior for Samaritans!

Still later, Jesus healed 10 lepers along the border between Samaria and Galilee. Nine of them hurried off to enjoy their restored health. The tenth alone came to Jesus "praising God in a loud voice." Then the newly cleansed man "threw himself at Jesus' feet and thanked him."

Luke adds pointedly, "And he was a Samaritan!"

Again, Jesus made sure His disciples did not miss the cross-cultural significance of the occasion, He asked: "Were not all ten cleansed? Where are the other nine? Was no one found to return and give praise to God except this foreigner?" (see Luke 17:11-19).

Jesus' penchant for holding up non-Jews as examples of righteousness for Jews—who, of all people on Earth, were supposed to be leaders in righteousness—is even more dramatically illustrated, however, by His Good Samaritan story, narrated in response to a question by a testy, self-justifying expert in Jewish law! The question was, "Who is my neighbor?"

"A man was going down from Jerusalem to Jericho," Jesus began, "when he fell into the hands of robbers. They stripped him of his clothes, beat him and went away, leaving him half dead. A priest happened to be going down the same road, and when he saw the man, he passed by on the other side. . . . But a Samaritan [imagine the expression on that legal "expert's" face beginning to sour] as he traveled, came where the man was; and when he saw him, he took pity on him. He went to him and bandaged his wounds, pouring on oil and wine. Then he put the man on his own donkey, took him to an inn and took care of him" (Luke 10:30-34).

Telling stories like that, Jesus could hardly be accused of currying favor with His fellow Jews! In fact, multitudes of people through the centuries have viewed His absolutely consistent refusal to stoop to political expediency as one of the surest evidences for His sinlessness! Muhammad, as I discuss in my book *Secrets of the Koran*, tragically and utterly failed this test.

Here is another instance in which Jesus pushed directly against the stream of popular prejudice in His time. "Now he had to go through Samaria," reads an account in John's Gospel. "So he came to a town in

Samaria called Sychar . . . Jacob's well was there and Jesus . . . sat down by the well. . . . When a Samaritan woman came to draw water, Jesus said to her, 'Will you give me a drink?' . . . The Samaritan woman said to him, 'You are a Jew and I am a Samaritan woman. How can you ask me for a drink?'"

From that seemingly unpromising beginning, Jesus went on to pierce the armor of that Samaritan woman's resistance to everything Jewish. He even managed to make the statement "salvation is from the Jews" and get away with it! The Samaritan woman believed Him. Totally enthused, she left her water jar by the well, ran into Sychar, rallied the townsfolk and brought them en masse to meet Jesus.

Meanwhile His disciples, who had been shopping for food in Sychar, were shocked upon their return to see Jesus conversing with a woman, let alone a *Samaritan* woman! They themselves while shopping in Sychar had been careful to keep everything on a "business only" basis even with Samaritan men! For as John explains in his account, "Jews have no dealings with Samaritans."

Still they hesitated to criticize Jesus. They just frowned and said, "Rabbi, eat something."

"I have food to eat that you know nothing about," Jesus replied. While they were wondering what He meant, the Samaritan woman reappeared, leading a host of her fellow Sycharians to Jesus. Perhaps nodding toward the Samaritans, Jesus continued, "My food . . . is to do the will of him who sent me and to finish his work" (see John 4:4-34).

And what is the will and work of Yahweh? To make His promise to Abraham come true—including that "bottom line" about all peoples on Earth being blessed through Abraham's descendants! And as Jesus saw that crowd of Samaritans coming toward Him, He knew His promise to Abraham was one step closer to being fulfilled. Another people was coming in!

Swaying as they walked like ripe wheat heads in the wind, the Samaritans reminded Jesus of a field of grain. "Open your eyes and look at the fields!" He told His disciples. "They are ripe for harvest" (v. 35). Samaritans? Wheat for God's harvest? Some wheat! many Jews would have scoffed. *Weeds* perhaps, but not wheat! But in the eyes of Jesus,

Messiah for all peoples, Samaritans could be wheat!

One day Jesus proclaimed, ever so provocatively, that three Gentile cities—Tyre, Sidon and even disreputable Sodom—would fare better on the day of judgment than three Jewish cities named Korazin, Bethsaida and Capernaum! Why? Because the Gentile cities mentioned, had they witnessed the miracles Jesus performed in Galilee, would have "repented long ago sitting in sackcloth and ashes" (Luke 10:13).

Likewise He warned Jews of His time that Gentile men of Nineveh would "stand up at the judgment with this generation and condemn it!" Why? "They repented at the preaching of Jonah, and now one greater than Jonah is here!" (Matt. 12:41).

In the same vein, Jesus warned His contemporaries that the Gentile "Queen of the South" would "rise at the judgment with this generation and condemn it!" On what basis? "She came from the ends of the earth to listen to Solomon's wisdom, and now one greater than Solomon is here" (Matt. 12:41-42).

Luke is the chronicler who records for us how intensely Jews in Jesus' time resented this particular sort of comparison.

People in Nazareth, Jesus' own hometown, had heard astonishing reports detailing miracles He worked in other places. Every Nazarene, we may be sure, stood tiptoe with expectation when at last Jesus returned to Nazareth for the first time since He began to display His previously unsuspected talent for working wonders. If He lavished so many miracles on strangers, who could guess what wonders He might perform for His own townsfolk!

Folks said He had so many miracles in Him He could even afford to waste some on Gentiles and Samaritans! He would have to exert Himself in a very special way among His own Jewish acquaintances to make up for that! Luke tells us what happened: "On the Sabbath day he went into the synagogue, as was his custom. And he stood up to read. The scroll of the prophet Isaiah was handed to him. Unrolling it, he found the place where it is written: 'The Spirit of the Lord is upon me, because he has anointed me to preach good news to the poor.'"

One can imagine Jesus emphasizing the word "poor" and then looking around to take the measure of this audience of people who considered themselves so deserving of special privilege. He continued reading: "'He has sent me to proclaim freedom for the prisoners . . . '" Did He utter that word "prisoners" in a manner that suddenly charged it with a meaning far wider than just "jailbirds"? "' . . . And recovery of sight for the *blind*, to release the *oppressed*, to proclaim the year of the Lord's favor'" (Luke 4:16-19, emphasis added; see also Isa. 61:1-2).

While the weight of Isaiah's profound statement was still settling upon his fellow Nazarenes, Jesus "rolled up the scroll, gave it back to the attendant and sat down. The eyes of everyone in the synagogue," Luke adds suspensefully, "were fastened on him, and he said to them, 'Today this scripture is fulfilled in your hearing'" (vv. 20-21). Whispers of approval rustled through the synagogue. "All spoke well of him," Luke wrote, "and were amazed at the gracious words that came from his lips" (v. 22).

That, of course, was because they still did not understand why He chose to read that particular passage from Isaiah. No matter; they were so eager to see Him work miracles that they hardly cared to ponder the meaning of His speech. His words were simply a prelude to His miracles, were they not? Of course! Miracles must be the main business of the day.

"Surely," Jesus continued, "you will quote this proverb to me: 'Physician heal yourself! Do here in your home town what we have heard that you did in Capernaum!' I tell you the truth . . . no prophet is accepted in his home town" (vv. 23-24).

This latter sentence, spoken very likely with a sigh, was but a transition to the solemn point of His text. To illustrate what Isaiah meant when he foreshadowed Messiah as ministering selectively to people who were poor, imprisoned, blind or oppressed, Jesus drew masterfully upon two other well-known Old Testament narratives. The first: "There were many widows in Israel in Elijah's time, when . . . there was a severe famine throughout the land. Yet Elijah was not sent to any of them, but to a widow of Zarephath in the [Gentile] region of *Sidon*" (vv. 25-26, emphasis added).

If air inside the synagogue turned sour with this first illustration, it actually curdled with the second: "There were many in Israel with leprosy in the time of Elisha the prophet, yet not one of them was cleansed—only Naaman the *Syrian*" (v. 27, emphasis added).

Hell broke loose. "All the people in the synagogue were furious when they heard this," Luke recorded. "They got up, drove him [not merely out of the synagogue but even] out of the town." Still not satisfied, they took Him "to the brow of the hill on which the town was built, in order to throw him down the cliff. But he walked right through the crowd and went on his way" (vv. 28-30).

So much for Jewish interest in the bottom line of their own Abrahamic Covenant! The suggestion that Yahweh might even bypass needy Jews to fulfill that special clause for Gentiles was totally obnoxious and unacceptable, even if it could be supported with Scripture! How lonely Jesus must have felt to be perhaps the only one in the entire Jewish nation who cared about the full text of Yahweh's ancient covenant with Abraham! And how hard it must have been to keep trying to share that lonely vision with people who should have been interested, but weren't.

Even His own disciples took, as we shall see, decades to comprehend Jesus' "all-peoples" perspective. Yet how patiently Jesus bore their seemingly endless rejection of this, His most far-reaching and deeply compassionate design. How patiently He still waits for our full compliance with that design today! He had, of course, to keep working toward that end. It was His mission. And it still involves His personal 4,000-year-old commitment to God and to Abraham.

And Jesus alone knew how wistfully peoples like the Karen, the Lahu, the Wa, the Lisu, the Kachin, the Mizo, the Naga, the Gedeo, the Santal, the Incas and thousands of others were waiting. He would not fail them (or us!) by letting that vision die. But there was an even stronger reason which caused Him to persist.

Immediately after the near sacrifice of Isaac, Yahweh confirmed His covenant with Abraham with that famous oath! Notice: "I swear by myself, declares the Lord, that because you [Abraham] have done this and have not withheld your son, your only son, I will surely bless you . . . and through your offspring all nations on earth will be blessed, because you have obeyed me" (Gen. 22:15-18).

The writer of the New Testament letter to the Hebrews comments on the above Genesis passage as follows: "When God made his promise to Abraham, since there was no one greater for him to swear by, he swore by himself. . . . *Because God wanted to make the unchanging nature of his purpose very clear to the heirs of what was promised, he confirmed it with an oath.* God did this so that, by two unchangeable things in which it is impossible for God to lie, we who have fled to take hold of the hope offered to us may be greatly encouraged. We have this hope as an anchor for the soul, firm and secure" (Heb. 6:13-19, emphasis added).

There was no way, then, that Jesus the Messiah could have abandoned the "all-peoples imperative"! God had already staked His very name and character upon its fulfillment! What's more, His very name and character are still staked upon the fulfillment of that imperative today! Anyone who does not understand this cannot possibly understand what God is doing in history.

Not only in small towns like Nazareth, but also in the big city of Jerusalem, Jesus' unswerving loyalty to the "all-peoples imperative" kept Him in constant tension with His fellow Jews. Matthew, Mark and Luke all record that Jesus, near the end of His ministry, entered what was almost certainly the court of the Gentiles—one of the precincts of Herod's famous Temple at Jerusalem. Why was it called the court of the Gentiles? There was only one reason—it was the only part of the Temple designed exclusively to remind Jews of their ancient obligation to honor the bottom line of the Abrahamic Covenant! Apart from that courtyard, Jews might more easily forget that they were blessed to be a blessing—to Gentiles!

It was also the only part of the Temple that Gentile tourists or even devout Gentile "God-fearers" were allowed to enter. It was God's purpose that Gentiles entering that sacred precinct would hear Jews praying for them, and would know unmistakably that the God of the Jews was truly the God of the whole earth, a God who desired to bless all peoples.

To His utter indignation, Jesus found the court of the Gentiles dedicated instead to Jewish commercial enterprise. Oxen and sheep pens, dove cages and moneychangers with their scales and abacuses filled the court of the Gentiles from gate to wall. Clatter and clutter, niggling and haggling were everywhere—more noxious perhaps than even the stench of animal dung.

Originally, Temple-related enterprises of this type—if they existed at all—were located outside the Temple precinct. Then, gradually, businessmen realized how much greater their profits would be if only they could be nearer to the inner court of the Temple where animals were actually sacrificed. It occurred to them that the area called the court of the Gentiles was not really being put to much use. After all, who really prays for Gentiles any more? And if anyone wants to pray for Gentiles, he can do it anywhere. Was it really practical to tie up an entire area of high-potential real estate for a pursuit as unpopular as praying for Gentiles? "Rezone the court of the Gentiles for commercial use!" thus became a popular campaign issue. Eventually, the proposal won the day and became law—with perhaps a shekel or two passing under the high priest's office desk.

In came the animal sellers, followed by the moneychangers, eager to exploit Gentile visitors who came to the Temple. Visitors from afar, unfamiliar with currency exchange rates in Palestine, might not know when a money changer was ripping them off through an unfair rate of exchange, not to mention an inaccurate balance scale.

Jesus saw it all and took action. He "drove out all who were buying and selling there. He overturned the tables of the money changers and the benches of those selling doves" (Matt. 21:12). To those who shouted, "Just what do you think you are doing?" Jesus responded not so much with angry denunciation as with teaching based upon Scripture.

What did He teach to justify His decisive action against His fellow Jews' vile prostitution of the court of the Gentiles? He chose a masterful combination of quotes from two Old Testament prophets. The first came from Isaiah: "My house [God's temple] will be called a house of prayer for all nations" (Mark 11:17; see also Isa. 56:7). Then Jesus placed a phrase from Jeremiah in tandem: "But you have made it 'a den of robbers!'" (see Jer. 7:11).

The context of His quotation from Isaiah bears strong relationship to the "all-peoples imperative" of the Abrahamic Covenant. For in that context, Isaiah quotes Yahweh as saying: "Let no foreigner who has joined himself to the Lord say, 'The Lord will surely exclude me from his people' . . . and foreigners who bind themselves to the Lord to serve him, to love the name of the Lord, and to worship him, . . . these I will bring to my holy mountain and give them joy in my house of prayer. Their burnt offerings and sacrifices will be accepted on my altar; for my house will be called a house of prayer for all nations" (Isa. 56:3,6-7).

Let all Gentiles take note that Jesus drove out the moneychangers not merely to defend the sanctity of the Temple itself, but also to defend our right to have our spiritual need represented in it! Moreover, that act cost Him dearly, for "the chief priests and the teachers of the law [who probably sold commercial franchises to those money changers, or at least agreed with those who did] heard this and began looking for a way to kill him, for they feared him, because the whole crowd was amazed at his teaching" (Mark 11:18).

Such blatant rejection of the profoundly open spirit of the Abrahamic Covenant caused Jesus to extend a grim warning to Jewish leaders. The first portent of that warning came the very day after He cleansed the Temple. Spending the night in Bethany . . .

"Early in the morning, as he was on his way back to the city, he was hungry. Seeing a fig tree by the road, he went up to it but found nothing on it except leaves. Then he said to it, 'May you never bear fruit again!' Immediately the tree withered. When the disciples saw this, they were amazed" (Matt. 21:18-20).

The real point of this incident did not emerge, however, until later that day. As Jesus taught in the Temple, jealous Jewish leaders glowered on the edges of the crowd, racking their brains for some way to upstage Him. Jesus, however, took the initiative against them with various parables, including one about a landowner (Yahweh) who planted a vineyard (Israel), rented it out to tenant farmers (Jewish religious leaders) and went on a journey. After harvest, he sent his servants (the prophets) to collect his share of the crop (their obedience to the conditions of his covenant) as rent. The tenant farmers beat, stoned or killed all the landowner's servants. Finally, the landowner used his ultimate persuasion—he sent his own son. But the tenant farmers killed him too!

"What," Jesus asked, "will the owner of the vineyard do to those tenants?"

"He will bring those wretches to a wretched end," the Jews replied, "and he will rent the vineyard to other tenants, who will give him his share of the crop at harvest time."

Jesus replied: "Therefore I tell you that the kingdom of God will be taken away from you and given to a people who will produce its fruit" (see Matt. 21:33-43). Surely Jesus' disciples must have remembered immediately the incident of the fig tree which withered under His curse because it provided no fruit when He approached it! Clearly, they must have guessed that the withered fig tree foreshadowed a tragedy soon to befall Israel itself!

No warning could possibly be plainer—Yahweh was about to table the spiritual franchise once entrusted to the Jews and open a new administration among Gentile peoples who were willing to honor the spirit of the Abrahamic Covenant! But just in case they missed the point, Jesus followed this parable immediately with a second.

A king (Yahweh) prepared a banquet for his son's wedding and invited his friends (the Jews). They, however, totally rejected his invitation, even to the extent of abusing or slaying some of the servants the king sent as bearers of the invitation! The king's response was twofold: First, he sent an army to punish the wretches who abused or slew his servants; Second, he sent still other servants out into streets and lanes to gather masses of previously unprivileged people (Gentiles) to enjoy the banquet with him. Thus our Lord foreshadowed an impending invitation of Yahweh's grace soon to be extended to Samaritans and to Gentiles of every stripe through the ministry of His own apostles and their successors!

Missiologist Ralph Winter once startled an audience by affirming, "Jesus did not come to *give* the Great Commission! He came to take it away—from the Jews who had already possessed it in prototype for nearly two thousand years and had done almost nothing with it! It was time for the world to see what believing Gentiles, entrusted with that same imperative in New Testament form, would do with it."

The idea that Yahweh might punish their gross disobedience by annulling their spiritual franchise for an age or two was, to the Jews, unthinkable! How mad Jesus must have seemed to suggest such an incredible thing! Yet their own lawgiver, Moses, had already warned of that very possibility! "They made me jealous by what is no god," he quotes Yahweh as saying, "I will make them envious by those who are not a people" (Deut. 32:21, quoted by Paul in Rom. 10:19).

What was the immediate response of the Jewish leaders to Jesus' warnings? "They looked for a way to arrest him because they knew he had spoken the parable against them" (Mark 12:12). Some of them, however, skilled in debate through rabbinical training, tried to trick Jesus into verbalizing political impropriety against Rome. Alas for His interrogators, He handled this and other questions with the ease of a veteran infielder scooping up grounders and catching the runner at first every time!

What was their question? "Is it right to pay taxes to Caesar or not?" (Matt. 22:17). What would Jesus, the man for all peoples, advise in the extremely sensitive matter of Jews paying taxes to a *Gentile* emperor?

He began His reply: "You hypocrites, why are you trying to trap me?" On what basis did He call them hypocrites? Simply this—they professed to stand for both the Abrahamic Covenant and its later extensions in the Law of Moses and the Prophets, yet they frustrated the intent of that Covenant in almost every vital way!

Jesus continued: "'Show me the coin used for paying the tax.' They brought him a denarius, and he asked them, 'Whose portrait is this? And whose inscription?' 'Caesar's,' they replied. Then he said to them, 'Give to Caesar what is Caesar's, and to God what is God's'" (vv. 18-21).

With these words, Jesus the Messiah for all peoples, acknowledged the right of even unbelieving Gentile kings to reign over the Jews, presumably until a period He later called "the times of the Gentiles" was fulfilled (see Luke 21:24).

His enemies were "unable to trap him," wrote Luke. "Astonished by his answer, they became silent" (Luke 20:26).

Meanwhile Jesus, though still ministering blessings to Jews on every hand (as required by the "top line" of the Abrahamic Covenant), kept informing His disciples that they themselves must shortly minister to Gentiles as well. Once, for example, He sent them out on a training mission explaining that although at the moment He was sending them, not to Gentiles or Samaritans, but to "the lost sheep of Israel," later they would be "brought before governors and kings as witnesses to them and *to the Gentiles!*" (Matt. 10:5-6,18, emphasis added).

Jesus most likely placed this temporary restriction upon His disciples, not to encourage disregard for Gentiles and Samaritans, but because His disciples were still spiritually and mentally unprepared to undertake a cross-cultural mission.

Later Jesus, explaining metaphors from His now famous Parable of the Weeds to His disciples, identified the "field" in the parable as "the world," not just Israel (see Matt. 13:24-30,36-43).

In the same context, Jesus dropped a one-sentence parable about a woman who mixed yeast into a large amount of flour and let it "work all through the dough" (Matt. 13:33). By analogy with Jesus' own interpretation of the Parable of the Weeds, the large amount of flour in this mini parable seems also to designate the world, and the yeast accordingly becomes the gospel's pervasive witness throughout the entire world.

Elsewhere Jesus forewarned His disciples that the end of the age could not happen until the gospel had first been "preached to all nations" (Mark 13:10). The Greek phrase *ta ethne* should, according to many scholars, be translated "all peoples," rather than "all nations," which erroneously implies that divine interest centers upon transitory political structures rather than ethnically distinct human communities. India, for example, is one "nation," but India embraces 3,500 "peoples." One would have to say there are 3,500 Indias, if *ethne* is translated as "nations."

Later on, some Greeks came to a feast at Jerusalem and sought audience with Jesus. Philip and Andrew, two of Jesus' disciples, relayed the request to Jesus who, as usual, exploited the occasion to get another wedge in for the "all-peoples perspective": "But I, when I am lifted up from the earth, will draw *all men* to myself" (John 12:32, emphasis added). This prophecy foreshadowed the manner of Jesus' death— crucifixion! But it also foretold the effect! All men—not merely in spite of Jesus' humiliation, but because of it—would be drawn to Him as God's anointed deliverer. On the surface this statement could be interpreted to mean that everyone in the world will become a Christian. Since we know that this is quite unlikely, the statement probably means instead that some of all kinds of men will be drawn to Jesus when they learn that His death atoned for their sins. And that is exactly what the Abrahamic Covenant promised—not that all people would be blessed, but that all peoples would be represented in the blessing. Jesus' disciples thus gained still another fair warning of the Great Commission soon to follow!

Jesus' keen preoccupation with the future evangelization of Gentile peoples emerged in still another context through an indirect statement. When Mary, a devout woman, poured a jar of very expensive perfume on Jesus' feet, symbolically anointing Him beforehand for burial, Judas Iscariot rebuked her for wasting expensive ointment (see John 12:4-5). Jesus Himself took up Mary's defense. Explaining her motivation, He added a comment that revealed much about His own deep inner purpose: "Wherever the gospel is preached throughout the world, what she has done will also be told, in memory of her" (Mark 14:9).

Immediately afterward, Judas Iscariot slipped away and secretly arranged to betray Jesus to His enemies. Egocentric Judas by that time was totally disenchanted with his Lord. Jesus' indifference to the possibility of using His power for the political and monetary enrichment of His disciples had brought Judas to the end of his patience. And now, as if to add insult to injury, Jesus had embarrassed Judas openly by endorsing Mary's costly act of worship after Judas had criticized it. This proved to Judas—if he still had any doubts—that Jesus simply did not have a gift for financial management!

Finally, from Judas's ethnocentric viewpoint, Jesus' soaring ambition to dissipate Messianic blessings over the entire Gentile world (instead of concentrating the blessing among Jews where it could really count for something) must have seemed entirely impractical! Apparently Judas saw at last that Jesus really was serious about throwing the banquet hall of Jewish privilege open to Gentile dogs! If so, then Judas may have been the most intelligent of the 12 disciples, because the other 11, as we shall see, took much longer to take that emphasis of Jesus' ministry seriously.

Both Judas's clash with Jesus over the value of Mary's act of worship and Jesus' reassertion of the "all-peoples perspective" in His defense of Mary seem related in Scripture as catalysts precipitating Judas's decision to betray Jesus! This apparently was for Judas the final offense that shredded the last vestige of any obligation he still felt toward Jesus.

Suddenly Judas began adding up his score of grievances. He had

invested three years of his life hoping to help Jesus set up and adminis-
ter the new Messianic Corporation. Still, apart from some "advances" he
had "borrowed" from the corporation treasury, he was not the least bit
better off financially for all his trouble! For that matter, Jesus' far out
(literally) management policies aimed at incorporating Gentile peoples
into His plans gave not the slightest promise of any financial reward in
the future either!

Judas began to feel sorry for himself. Was there no way he could
compensate himself for at least some of the wages he had forfeited to
follow Jesus during that financially disappointing three-year period?

Suddenly Judas thought of a clever way to regain at least part of his
losses. It would require him to betray a friend, of course, but that friend
had already demonstrated a remarkable ability to live with danger and
survive. There was no chance, Judas thought, that a secret little deal with
the chief priests would actually result in Jesus' death! Either Jesus would
outwit His accusers in court (He was great with words), or else the same
crowds who welcomed Jesus in His triumphal entry would demand His
release on threat of riot (He was incredibly popular at the moment!).
Failing that, Jesus Himself could easily cheat death by some miraculous
escape. True, Jesus predicted on several occasions that He would eventually come to a tragic end; but this was surely not the time. He was still in
His prime. His ministry was at its apex. The chief priests would arrest
Him, of course, but then they would soon be forced by popular opinion
to release Him.

Judas, meanwhile, would slip away to some other part of Palestine
with 30 pieces of silver to invest in a bright new future! But not until he
had lingered in Jerusalem just long enough to see how Jesus' release
would happen!

To Judas's utter horror, it didn't happen that way!

From the moment of the arrest, things started going wrong. Jesus
inexplicably stopped exercising His marvelous powers of argument to
outwit His enemies. The man who had foiled the most potent debaters
of Judaism now stood incredibly tongue-tied before Annas, Caiaphas,
Pilate and Herod, saying hardly a word in His own defense. Likewise,
Judas listened in vain for some news that Jesus had at last exploited His

awesome miraculous powers to slip through the fingers of His enemies. And when the sentence of death was announced, even the crowds did not rise to His defense! Impossibly gullible people, some of whom had welcomed Jesus as Messiah only days earlier, now allowed professional agitators to persuade them to clamor for Jesus' crucifixion!

Crucifixion?! Judas must have gasped! Jesus? Pierced with iron nails? Dying in agony upon a Gentile cross? That was a method of torture reserved only for the foulest criminals! That was not supposed to happen! Or was it? Perhaps the betrayer recalled in that moment Jesus' words: "And I, if I be lifted up from the earth . . ." The words had seemed at the time to refer to some future state of exaltation. Now, too late, the real meaning was beginning to emerge. And Judas knew that he—one of Jesus' original 12 disciples—had contributed to this awesomely unjust crime! Matthew the apostle describes Judas's reaction to this unexpected turn of events:

"When Judas, who betrayed him, saw that Jesus was condemned, he was seized with remorse and returned the thirty silver coins to the chief priests and the elders. 'I have sinned,' he said, 'for I have betrayed innocent blood.' 'What is that to us?' they replied . . . So Judas threw the money into the temple . . . Then he went away and hanged himself" (Matt. 27:3-5).

What finally happened to those 30 pieces of silver? Interestingly, the chief priests picked them up and used them to buy a potter's field, which they then converted into a cemetery for guess who? Gentiles! Jewish law prohibited the burial of Gentiles in Jewish cemeteries, but Jesus, even through the money paid for His betrayal, in effect made provision for them (see Matt. 27:6-10).

The crucifixion, meanwhile, took place in that same "region of Moriah" where Abraham—1,900 years before—once stood prepared to offer his only son, the innocent Isaac, at God's command. This time, however, there was no "ram caught in a thicket" to take the place of the innocent Son. Instead, the ancient prophecy—"in the mountain of the Lord it will be provided"—was fulfilled.

And Jesus Christ was that provision. John, one of His disciples, later realized the significance of what happened that day, and wrote: "Jesus

Christ, the Righteous One, . . . is the atoning sacrifice for our sins, and not only for ours but also for the sins of the whole world" (1 John 2:1-2).

This, then, was the first of the blessings which Abraham's singular Descendant would share, not only with Jews like John, but with "the whole world"!

As Jesus hung upon that cross, an inscription in Aramaic, the language used by most Palestinian Jews of that day, was nailed above His head: "Jesus of Nazareth, the King of the Jews." But that inscription was written also in two other Gentile languages, Latin and Greek!

And at the very moment when Jesus cried aloud, "Father, into your hands I commit my spirit," a Gentile soldier was standing near the base of the cross. He saw Jesus breathe His last. His comment? "Surely this was a righteous man" (Luke 23:46-47).

Just as the disciples still did not believe Jesus' intimations of Gentile evangelism, so also they never really believed Him when He said He would rise from the dead. He surprised them on both counts! Three days after His entombment He resurrected! And one of His first encounters after resurrection began in incognito fashion with two of His disciples on a road leading to Emmaus (see Luke 24:13-49). During the opening exchange the two disciples, still not recognizing Jesus, complained: "We had hoped that [Jesus] was the one who was going to redeem Israel" (v. 21); they did not add, "and make Israel a blessing to all peoples." A blind spot in their hearts still effectively obscured that part of the Abrahamic Covenant.

"How foolish you are," Jesus responded, "and how slow of heart to believe all that the prophets have spoken! Did not the Christ have to suffer these things and then enter his glory?" (vv. 25-26).

Then, beginning with the five "books of Moses and all the Prophets, he explained to them what was said in all the Scriptures concerning himself." He had covered much of that ground before, but He went over it again—patiently (see v. 27). And this time, the two disciples' hearts burned within them as He opened the Scriptures (see v. 32). Was a wider perspective at last winning its way into their hearts?

Later they recognized Jesus but at the same moment He vanished from their sight! They retraced their steps at once to Jerusalem, found the Eleven (as the disciples were called for a while after Judas's defection) and recounted their experience. But before they finished talking, Jesus Himself appeared among them, and the Eleven experienced the end of the story for themselves!

As unerringly as a swallow returning to its nest, Jesus returned to the Scriptures and their central theme: "Then he opened their minds so they could understand the Scriptures. He told them, 'This is what is written: The Christ will suffer and rise from the dead on the third day, *and repentance and forgiveness of sins will be preached in his name to all nations* [i.e. *ethne*—peoples], beginning at Jerusalem. You are witnesses of these things'" (Luke 24:45-48, emphasis added).

Notice, however, that He still did not command them to go. That would come a few days later, on a mountain in Galilee where—as far as the disciples were concerned—it all started. And here is the wording of the command which the Abrahamic Covenant had already foreshadowed for 2,000 years, and which Jesus for three long years had been preparing His disciples to receive: "All authority in heaven and on earth has been given to me. *Therefore go and make disciples of all nations*, baptizing them in the name of the Father and of the Son and of the Holy Spirit, and teaching them to obey [note the limitation that follows] everything I have commanded you. And surely I will be with you always, to the very end of the age" (Matt. 28:18-20, emphasis added).

It was not an unfair command. The Old Testament foreshadowed it. Jesus' daily teaching anticipated it. His frequent prejudice-free ministry among both Samaritans and Gentiles had given the disciples a real-life demonstration of how to carry it out. Now He added the promise of His own authority bequeathed and His own presence in company—if they obeyed!

Still later, moments before He ascended back into heaven from the Mount of Olives (near Bethany), He added a further promise: "You will receive power when the Holy Spirit comes on you; and you will be my witnesses . . ." Then followed Jesus' famous formula for the exocentric progression of the gospel: ". . . in Jerusalem, and in all Judea and Samaria, *and to the ends of the earth*" (Acts 1:8, emphasis added).

It was Jesus' last command. Without another word, and without waiting for any discussion of the proposal, He ascended into heaven to await His followers' complete obedience to it!

Jesus knew of course that there was no hope of rescuing the majority of Jews in His time from blind self-centeredness any more than there is ever much hope of rescuing the majority of any people, for that matter, from the same plight! Throughout history the majority of Jews focused so exclusively upon the top line of the Abrahamic Covenant that the bottom line became virtually invisible to them. It is probably not an exaggeration to describe their minds as hermetically sealed against any serious consideration of "the bottom line." That is why many Jews were determined to exploit Jesus' miraculous powers exclusively for their own benefit. But His covenant-based, all-peoples perspective clashed constantly with their own "our people" mentality. Even one of His disciples, as we have seen, betrayed Him in the context of this issue! The only hope, then, lay with these other 11. If only Jesus could win them to the all-peoples perspective, the full promise to Abraham, and not just a truncated version, could still be fulfilled.

Question! Could even the Son of Man—without negating human free will—transform 11 men whose thought patterns had been programmed from childhood to be extremely *ethnocentric*? The question may seem silly. Could not the Son of Man, who is also the omnipotent Son of God, do anything? The answer is yes, but—human free will implies God's prior decision not to tamper with the metaphysical base of that free will. It also implies man's ability to reject the persuasion God uses to influence that free will while leaving its metaphysical base intact!

Persuasion, not compulsion, is what even He must rely upon! And persuasion, by its very definition, must be resistible! Yet the God who thus renders Himself resistible is so intelligent that He can overrule every consequence of His own self-limitation with ease! Working around and even through human resistance as easily as through response, He still achieves His own eternal goals!

Ultimate suspense, then, does not hang upon the eventual success of God's design; for that success is assured. Ultimate suspense hangs rather upon questions like, *Who* among the sons and daughters of men will recognize the day of God's privilege when it dawns around them? And which men and women, among those who discern that privilege, will choose to scorn it as Esau scorned his birthright? And finally, just how will God accomplish His goal when even the men and women who love Him and make His purpose theirs turn out to be spiritually vulnerable, physically weak and oh-so-limited in understanding?

Can any other questions generate more suspense than these?

With that suspense heavy upon us, we shall now see how Jesus' all-out effort to change 11 clannish Jews into cross-cultural apostles fared. Incredibly, this, His finest and most strategic training effort, floated belly up in defeat until . . . Ah, but let us not get ahead of our story!

CHAPTER 7

The Hidden Message of Acts

Hundreds of millions of Christians think that Luke's Acts of the Apostles records the 12 apostles' obedience to the Great Commission. Actually it records their reluctance to obey it.

As the Eleven stood rooted to that hilltop, watching Jesus vanish into a cloud, did they really feel positive response to that last command? Surely Jesus' example of compassion for a Roman centurion, a Syrophoenician mother, a Samaritan leper, a Gadarene demoniac, a Syrian general like Naaman, the widow of Zarephath, the men of Nineveh who repented, and the people of Sodom and Gomorrah who perished without a clear call to repentance—must now prove sufficient to melt prejudice from their hearts, replace that prejudice with "peoples consciousness," and send them on their way to the ends of the earth!

Surely His sweeping survey of the Scriptures followed by His direct command, unveiling God's plan for the whole world, must now provide the disciples with adequate motivation! And finally—would not the promised bestowal of the Holy Spirit's power transform them into dynamic cross-cultural commandos?

But wait—regarding that bestowal of the Holy Spirit's power—suppose God had hired you as a public relations expert to plan the event for Him! Suppose He had given you just one specification—it must happen in a manner which will make absolutely clear to even the dullest disciple that the power about to be bestowed is not merely for the personal blessing or exaltation of the recipients, but rather to enable them to take the gospel across the world to all peoples!

Even if you were the most ingenious public relations consultant of all time, you probably would not have fantasized a clearer way to get that point across than the following.

When finally the power of the Holy Spirit came upon Jesus' disciples, the timing was perfect! God-fearing Jews from at least 15 different regions of the Near and Middle East had gathered in Jerusalem for a feast called Pentecost. In addition to their common knowledge of Hebrew and/or Aramaic, these strangers—often called Jews of the Diaspora, the "scattering"—spoke probably as many as several dozen Gentile languages.

The power of the Holy Spirit coming upon the apostles and other faithful followers of Jesus caused them to speak miraculously in the many Gentile languages represented by the throng of diaspora Jews and Gentile converts then gathered in Jerusalem. Why?

Not merely to bless those who spoke. The bestowal of miraculous ability to speak *non-Jewish* languages was superfluous if only their own blessing was intended!

Further, it was not merely to bless the diaspora Jews who understood those languages. If only their edification was intended either the Hebrew or the Aramaic language could have served as well.

Nor was the purpose to demonstrate the Holy Spirit's ability to perform amazing miracles.

Seen in the context of Jesus' ministry and His clearly articulated plans for the whole world, the bestowal of that miraculous outburst of *Gentile* languages could have only one main purpose: to make crystal clear that the Holy Spirit's power was and is bestowed with the specific goal of the evangelization of all peoples in view! Any attempt to exploit the power of the Holy Spirit for one's personal pleasure or aggrandizement, or to seek signs and miracles as ends in themselves, must appear to God as a misconstrual of His purpose.

Yet we sometimes still see Christians seek power and signs with no thought of committing themselves to the evangelization of all peoples!

But let us see if that first generation of Christians realized the significance of the Holy Spirit's gifts any better.

With the power of the Holy Spirit crackling through their witness, the apostles quickly crossed the first of the four thresholds Jesus mentioned—they evangelized Jerusalem—no problem! Their critics soon complained, "You have filled Jerusalem with your teaching" (Acts 5:28). The comment, "The number of disciples in Jerusalem increased rapidly" (Acts 6:7), was also soon recorded. By the end of the seventh chapter of the book of Acts we find, however, that all of the apostles and their thousands of converts are still clustered in Jerusalem. Twenty-five percent of the book of Acts was already history and, as far as the record shows, they were not even making plans to obey the rest of Jesus' last command!

Even God was getting impatient, if we understand correctly what follows. God, it appears, was willing to use extreme measures to keep His Son's gift to all mankind from ending up as the exclusive property of just one people—the Jews. God's solution was very simple, if painful: He scattered the Christians through persecution. The enemies who hounded Jesus' followers never dreamed they were fulfilling God's will: "A great persecution broke out against the church at Jerusalem, and all *except the apostles* were scattered throughout Judea and Samaria" (Acts 8:1, emphasis added).

In the light of Jesus' last command, should not at least some of the apostles have led the way? Apparently even persecution could not dislodge them from home base. "Those who had been scattered preached the word wherever they went. Philip [not the apostle Philip, but rather one of the seven laymen appointed earlier to wait on tables for the thousands of believers in Jerusalem, see Acts 6:5] went down into a city of

Samaria and proclaimed Christ there. . . . So there was great joy in that city" (Acts 8:4-8).

After Philip, a "layman" on a working vacation from his catering service in Jerusalem (see Acts 6:1-5), had broken the Samaritan ice for them, the apostles decided to send two of their number—Peter and John—to add further blessing to the revival already in progress.

It could not have been an easy mission for Peter and John, and perhaps it was not easy for Philip either. Their own culture had trained Jews to be Class A Samaritan-avoiders; "for Jews do not associate with Samaritans" (John 4:9). Samaritans, you see, worked from quite a different set of presuppositions. They did not even agree that Jerusalem—the Holy City of the Jews—was the center of the world! And their blood was mixed with Gentile blood! Straight Gentile would probably have been easier for Jews to stomach, but a mixture . . . how detestable!

Sumeria, perhaps even Siberia, might have presented an easier mission for men of Jewish background than distasteful Samaria.

Nevertheless, Peter and John began to feel enthused about cross-cultural ministry in that Samaritan city. So enthused were they that they "preached the gospel in many Samaritan villages" immediately afterward, but only on their way home to—guess where—Jerusalem (see Acts 8:25)!

Meanwhile, that same spunky layman named Philip was off like a first-century Green Beret commando for the Holy Spirit on still another cross-cultural mission! "An angel of the Lord said to Philip, 'Go south to the road—the desert road—that goes down from Jerusalem to Gaza.' So he started out, and on his way he met an Ethiopian eunuch, an important official in charge of all the treasury of Candace, queen of the Ethiopians. This man had gone to Jerusalem to worship" (vv. 26-27).

Here is still another scriptural example of a Gentile person who worshiped the one true God. The record does not even say that he was a convert to Judaism, as it does earlier in the case of "Nicholas from Antioch, a convert to Judaism" (Acts 6:5).

Philip, traveling down "the desert road"—the closest thing to a freeway in his day—noticed that the Ethiopian was "sitting in his chariot reading the book of Isaiah the prophet." Isaiah, incidentally, contains a directive concerning Cush—the upper Nile Valley— the very place where that Ethiopian eunuch was employed under Queen Candace: "Go, swift messengers, to a people tall and smooth-skinned" (the Dinka people of that region are among the tallest in the world, and the towering Watusi of central Africa are believed also to originate from Cush), "to a people feared far and wide, an aggressive nation of strange speech, whose land is divided by rivers" (Isa. 18:2,7).

Philip, as far as we know, was the first "swift messenger" who ever came close to fulfilling that strongly cross-cultural directive found in the very book from which the Ethiopian was reading.

The Ethiopian's attention, however, was riveted upon a different passage, one found in verse 7 of Isaiah 53: "He was led like a sheep to the slaughter, and as a lamb before the shearer is silent, so he did not open his mouth" (Acts 8:32).

The Ethiopian asked Philip, "'Tell me, please, who is the prophet talking about, himself or someone else?' Then Philip began with that very passage of Scripture and told him the good news about Jesus" (Acts 8:34-35). The Ethiopian believed, requested baptism that very day and "went on his way rejoicing" (v. 39). History indicates that he may have successfully prepared the way for the later establishment of thousands of Christian churches in the far-away Valley of the Nile.

Good work, Philip!

Parting from the eunuch, Philip took the next on-ramp north on the "desert road," preaching along the seacoast from Azotus to Caesarea.

As far as we know, even Philip went no further. But, as he earlier blazed a trail for Peter and John into Samaria, so now his travels north-ward along the coast through Lydda, Joppa and Caesarea also seem to have prepared the way again for Peter. For in Acts 9:32 to 11:18, we find Peter again following Philip's footprints. Peter was doing a great work to be sure, but he was still preaching Christ only where He had already been preached—with one outstanding exception!

While in Caesarea, Philip apparently missed a God-seeking Roman centurion named Cornelius. And so the mission to win Cornelius to faith in Christ fell to Peter. And what a trauma it was even for Spirit-filled Peter to try to convert a Roman! A vision intended to purge Peter of his anti-Gentile biases had to be repeated three times, but Peter got the point (see 10:9-23). His subsequent meeting with Cornelius is a poignant study of human prejudice gradually melting down through the sheer goodness of the gospel of Jesus Christ.

Peter summarized his preparation for encounter with a God-seeking Roman by saying, "I now realize how true it is that God does not show favoritism but accepts men from every nation who fear him and do what is right" (10:34-35).

And yet, as he began to preach to Gentile Cornelius and his household, Peter described the gospel as a "message God sent to the people of Israel, telling the good news of peace through Jesus Christ" (v. 36). He didn't even go on to mention what Jesus so clearly specified—that it was also good news for all peoples. In the next breath, though, perhaps because he saw disappointment register on the faces of his Gentile listeners, Peter acknowledged that Jesus Christ does have some relationship with Gentiles. He is, Peter admitted, "Lord of all" (v. 36).

Still later Peter articulated Jesus' last command for his Gentile listeners; but, oh, what a highly abridged version of the Great Commission it was! "He commanded us to preach to the people" (v. 42). It is not too hard to guess which "people" Peter instinctively meant.

Then, in spite of Peter's hang-ups, the Holy Spirit finally got him to say it: "All the prophets testify about him that *everyone* [unqualified] who believes in him receives forgiveness of sins through his name" (v. 43, emphasis added).

And at that moment the Holy Spirit overwhelmed Peter's wistful Gentile audience just as He overwhelmed believing Jews on the day of Pentecost and outcasts of Samaria who were awakened first by deacon Philip's ministry.

But oh! The lesson of Jesus' worldwide cross-cultural imperative was so hard for even His own handpicked apostles to learn! It still is for us today.

When Peter returned to Jerusalem, his fellow Christians of Jewish background criticized him—as he knew they would—saying, "You went into the house of uncircumcised men and ate with them" (Acts 11:3). After Peter explained how God had practically compelled him to enter that Roman household, his critics changed their attitudes and said, "*So then, God has even granted the Gentiles repentance unto life*" (v. 18, emphasis added). Apparently this was a brand-new realization just then crossing the thresholds of their minds.

One wonders what—prior to that moment—they thought the purpose of Jesus' last command was! Or how they supposed it could be obeyed "to the ends of the earth" without a Jew ever having to eat with a Gentile!

Still other Christians of Jewish background, driven from Jerusalem by persecution, traveled as far north as Phoenicia, Cyprus and Antioch. They also proclaimed the gospel. But the record says they were careful to communicate it "only to Jews" (Acts 11:19).

Some of them, however, sent from Cyprus and Cyrene, decided to try giving the same message to Gentiles. At last! you cry, a breakthrough in their thinking has occurred! But wait a minute. They chose not to proclaim the gospel to Gentiles in their own home areas of Cyprus and Cyrene where they themselves were known. They did it in Antioch, where presumably they were not so well known. Why? Could it be that they wanted to preserve—if confronted by criticism such as Peter experienced—the option of fleeing away to their own regions, leaving the pot to boil behind them?

Once again the Spirit of the Lord broke through. One gets the impression from the book of Acts that He was constantly waiting to do just that wherever and as soon as He could find Christians who were willing to confront Gentiles with the gospel. And so we read: "The Lord's hand was with them, and a great number of people believed and turned to the Lord" (v. 21).

One can almost detect a note of mild sarcasm in the sentence that follows: "News of this reached the ears of the church at Jerusalem" (v. 22).

The inspired writer could as easily have said, "News of this reached the church in Jerusalem." The metaphor "ears of the church" may be a gentle hint of Luke's (and the Holy Spirit's) bemused impatience with the still-too-narrow vision of the Church in Jerusalem. We must remember, too, that all 12 apostles (Mathias had replaced Judas) were still ensconced as heads of the church at Jerusalem. Hence the phrase "ears of the church" could as easily—but for Luke's gentle diplomacy—have been rendered "the ears of the apostles."

Nor did even one of the apostles venture to Antioch to see the great things happening among Gentile converts there. They sent a man named Barnabas. Why a deputy to Antioch?

Could it be that Peter, John and the rest were suffering from a common human affliction called "headquarters fever"?

They will always be Christ's apostles. Their names are written forever upon the 12 foundation stones of the New Jerusalem (see Rev. 21:14). And yet, just as the four Gospels deliberately expose many of their human failings—bickering over rank, impetuosity, trying to steer Jesus away from the cross and so on, so the book of Acts reveals another error just as serious—their reticence to take Christ's last command seriously, at least during the early years following Pentecost.

Why did they linger in Jerusalem year after year, instead of going with the power God had given them on bold cross-cultural probes to more distant peoples?

Perhaps the best justification for their delay was the need to get their heads together—while Jesus' words and deeds were still fresh in their collective memory—and compile the data from which Matthew, Mark, the Gentile Luke and John later wrote their four Gospels. This could have kept all of the apostles occupied for 5 to 10 years, and some of them perhaps longer. Evidence indicates, however, that 20 years or more passed before they began to move out.

Did they also think that their continuing presence in Jerusalem was necessary to guarantee that the Holy City would always be central to the new faith, as it was to Judaism? If so, they had clearly forgotten what Jesus once said to the Samaritan woman beside that old well at Sychar: "Believe me, woman, a time is coming when you will worship the Father neither on this mountain nor in Jerusalem" (John 4:21).

Or was it the fact that they took wives (see 1 Cor. 9:5) who couldn't travel such distances?

Or was it their old argument over who would be greatest that kept them cloistered in Jerusalem? To leave the large, well-established church in the Holy City and dirty one's hands in rough, potentially dangerous pioneer missionary work would be to step down in rank, wouldn't it? Did each apostle fear to leave Jerusalem in case one of the others might conspire during his absence to entrench himself as some sort of bishop of Jerusalem?

Whatever the answer or answers, clearly a new apostolic band was needed at once to rescue Jesus' last command from oblivion. Who on Earth could qualify to do what Jesus' own handpicked, Spirit-filled apostles were in large measure failing to do?

"Saul, Saul . . . why do you persecute me?"

It was the voice of the newly ascended Jesus, speaking out of a light shining brighter than the sun. Suddenly blinded by the light, Saul of Tarsus fell to the ground.

"Who are you, Lord?" he asked.

"I am Jesus, whom you are persecuting," came the reply, notably without threat of retaliation for that persecution. Saul winced. Not long before, he had guarded the coats of those who stoned Stephen, one of Jesus' most impassioned witnesses, and his conscience had bothered him ever since. For he had personally consented to Stephen's death and cast many others of Stephen's persuasion into prison—only to find now, to his own awe and shame—that everything they had said about their Lord was valid! Jesus must truly be Lord!

"Now get up and go into the city," the voice continued, "and you will be told what you must do" (see Acts 9:4-6).

While Saul, still blinded, waited for three days in Damascus, Jesus appeared to a humble believer named Ananias and sent him to heal the eyes of that decade's most notorious persecutor of Christians.

When Ananias hesitated, fearing for his own safety, Jesus said—note the words—"Go! This man is my chosen instrument to carry my name before the Gentiles and their kings and before the people of Israel. I will show him how much he must suffer for my name" (Acts 9:15).

Thus began the new apostolic band. Saul, admittedly, had certain advantages over the Palestine-born apostles for cross-cultural mission within the Roman Empire. He was raised in Tarsus, a predominantly Gentile city. He spoke not only Hebrew and Aramaic but also Greek and perhaps even Latin. He was born a Roman citizen. And his formal training in Old Testament Scriptures under the scholar Gamaliel enabled him to delineate the Old Testament moorings of Christian faith with unparalleled clarity and precision. Later Saul helped Barnabas teach that host of Gentile converts for one year at Antioch. By the end of that year, Saul had apparently forged a new, clearly denned policy for extending the gospel cross-culturally to Gentiles. Gentile converts, he decided under God, need not be circumcised as the law of Moses required for Jews. Nor need they necessarily be identified with Jewish synagogues. They could form their own *ecclesia*—churches—wherein they could worship God through Jesus Christ without having to weather the disapproving frowns and ceremonial structures of rigorous Judaists. From now on it would be the moral content of the law and not the ceremonial framework that mattered!

This was a major breakthrough. Up until that time, Peter and the other apostles had wrestled with the problem of how to make Gentile converts conform to the standards for admission to what were regarded as "Nazarene" synagogues. After all, what else was there for Gentile converts to join? And since official synagogues were not set up to accommodate large numbers of Gentile converts, it was embarrassing if large numbers of them came asking for admission. If too many were admitted, they might even become a majority! It was simply easier not to win them in the first place!

Saul's idea, which Barnabas apparently accepted, that Gentile converts could form their own self-perpetuating authoritative *ecclesia*—churches led not necessarily by Christian Jews, but by Gentile believers themselves—cleared the way for large numbers of Gentiles to come to Christ. And so, after one year ministering together at Antioch, Saul and Barnabas journeyed to Jerusalem to present their new model for Gentile evangelism to the apostles. Cautiously they selected only Peter, James and John, who "seemed to be leaders," for their first audience. The other apostles apparently were judged by Saul and Barnabas to be perhaps too closed-minded.

Saul took with him Titus—a Greek believer who had never been circumcised—as a test case. Peter, James and John—as Saul hoped—did not insist that Titus be circumcised (see Gal. 2:1-5). Gradually, one degree at a time, their attitudes were swinging around. Saul later wrote: "[Peter, James and John] added nothing to my message. On the contrary, they saw that I had been given the task of preaching the gospel to the Gentiles. . . . They agreed that we [Saul and Barnabas] should go to the Gentiles, and they to the Jews" (Gal. 2:6-7,9).

Notice the implication that none of the other apostles had yet ventured beyond the Jewish domain. Had any done so, Peter, James and John would hardly have spoken of Saul and Barnabas as the sole messengers of Christ to Gentiles.

How amazing! There were now at least 15 men generally recognized as apostles since Matthias, James the Lord's brother, and Saul and Barnabas joined the original 11. And yet, out of the 15, only 2 are "commissioned" to evangelize the estimated 900 million Gentiles in the world at that time. The other 13 are convinced that they are all needed to evangelize only about 3 million Jews, among whom there were already tens of thousands of witnessing believers! Their unashamed willingness to let Paul and Barnabas take on the entire Gentile world boggles the mind.

Was this what the Lord Jesus intended?

Saul, who around this time began to favor his Roman name, Paul, was not altogether very impressed with the other apostles. Little wonder! Paul wrote: "As for [Peter, James and John] who seemed to be important—whatever they were makes no difference to me; God does not judge by external appearance" (Gal. 2:6).

Later Paul even had an open confrontation with Peter in Antioch. In spite of Peter's experience with Cornelius, the Roman centurion through which the Lord went to great pains to teach Peter that it was all right for him to eat with Gentiles, Peter—though he had digested Cornelius's food—had still not fully digested the Holy Spirit's lesson. Paul describes the problem: "Before certain men came from James [the Lord's own brother!], [Peter] used to eat with the Gentiles. But when they arrived, he began to draw back and separate himself from the Gentiles because he was afraid of those who belonged to the circumcision group. The other Jews joined him in his hypocrisy . . . *even Barnabas* was led astray" (vv. 12-13, emphasis added). That's how grim the struggle to maintain an "all-peoples perspective" was!

Paul took decisive action: "When I saw that they were not acting in line with the truth of the gospel, I said to Peter in front of them all, 'You are a Jew, yet you live like a Gentile and not like a Jew. How is it, then, that you force Gentiles to follow Jewish customs?'" (v. 14). Paul explained his logic: "I do not set aside the grace of God, for if righteousness could be gained through the law, Christ died for nothing!" (v. 21).

With the hammering out of these new concepts on the anvil of Paul's experiences in Antioch, Jerusalem and Tarsus, the way was now cleared. Free at last from the hindrance of Jewish particularism, the gospel now could spread to thousands of different peoples as an intercultural spiritual force. It was in fact a message far too magnificent and openhearted to remain for long an ally of the bondage of pharisaic Judaism!

With the way thus cleared, "the Holy Spirit said, 'Set apart for me Barnabas and Saul for the work to which I have called them.' So after they had fasted and prayed, they (the church elders at Antioch—not the original apostles) placed their hands on them and sent them off" into the Gentile world (Acts 13:2-3).

Paul and Barnabas were fully assured that Gentiles who believe become "heirs together with Israel, members together of one body, and sharers together in *the promise* in Christ Jesus . . . and are no longer foreigners and aliens, but fellow citizens with God's people and members of God's household . . . a dwelling in which God lives by his Spirit" (Eph. 3:6; 2:19,22, emphasis added).

Paul would even dare to say, as he wrote later in his epistles, that in Christ "there is neither Jew nor Greek, slave nor free, male nor female . . . [but those who believe] are all one in Christ Jesus" (Gal. 3:28). For Christ "has destroyed the barrier, the dividing wall of hostility" (Eph. 2:14).

He and Barnabas later declared boldly: "We now turn to the Gentiles. For this is what the Lord has commanded us: 'I have made you a *light for the Gentiles*, that you may bring salvation to *the ends of the earth*'" (Acts 13:46-47, emphasis added).

The lines had been drawn. Christianity and Judaism were now separate religions! Peter, James and John had tried their utmost to keep them together, but the pressure of Jesus' last command was too strong. Spreading the blessing of Abraham to all peoples on Earth was still "the unchanging nature of his purpose." Once the Lord has placed Himself under oath He cannot and will not change His mind.

Paul and Barnabas later returned to churches in Antioch and reported that God had "opened the door of faith to the Gentiles" (Acts 14:27).

Later those churches sent Paul and Barnabas to Jerusalem on still a second occasion to sit down with Peter, James and John and try to settle once and for all a question still vexing many Jewish believers—must Gentile converts, in order to be saved, submit to the ordeal of circumcision and obey all points of the Law of Moses and its detailed rituals?

Peter, reconciled now to the inevitable, reminded the resulting council of his experience in Cornelius's household years earlier: "[God] made no distinction between us and them, for he purified their hearts by faith. Now then, why do you try to test God by putting on the necks of the disciples a yoke that neither we nor our fathers have been able to bear? No! We believe it is through the grace of our Lord Jesus that we are saved, just as they are" (Acts 15:9-11).

Later James, the Lord's brother, gave the last word: "[Peter] has described to us how God at first showed his concern by taking from the Gentiles a people for himself" (v. 14).

James put his finger on the main point—it was God's concern: it had to be, because they themselves could hardly have cared less! James continued: "The words of the prophets are in agreement with this, as it is written: 'After this I will return and rebuild David's fallen tent . . . that the remnant of men may see the Lord, and all the Gentiles who bear my name'" (vv. 15-17).

It is possible that some of the original apostles, Palestine-bound—at least until that conference—finally began to open their eyes at this point to the possibilities of ministry among faraway Gentiles. Hearing Paul and Barnabas report large scale response among Asian peoples may have forced them to realize at last that Jerusalem and Samaria were not the only places where the action was!

There is even a theory that Luke may have written his Acts of the Apostles as a subtly disguised handbook designed to encourage the other apostles and their Jewish converts to follow Paul's example in evangelizing the Gentiles!

In any case, Titus's destruction of Jerusalem in A.D. 70 must have scattered the apostles, since there was hardly a Jerusalem left to cloister in after that event.

Various traditions quoted by Early Church fathers and other sources indicate that: James the Just—Jesus' physical brother—never did leave Palestine, but was martyred in Jerusalem. However, the apostle John extended the apostle Paul's ministry in Asia Minor and died in the region of Smyrna and Ephesus. The apostle Peter extended his ministry into the Gentile world as far as Rome, and was crucified upside down by pagan Romans in that city.

Thomas, tradition says, allowed the bottom line of the Great Commission to lead him into "India." In those days India meant anything east of Syria; yet evidence indicates that Thomas may have penetrated all the way to the region of Madras, near the southern tip of India proper. A large number of very ancient churches in that region call themselves the *Mar Toma* churches. *Toma* may trace back to Thomas's name.

Andrew reportedly traveled north of the Black Sea among the wild tribes of Scythia—forefathers of many present-day peoples of northern Europe. Other apostles apparently penetrated Ethiopia, North Africa, Syria and possibly southern Arabia. Perhaps someday researchers will uncover ancient documents which will clarify with greater accuracy what finally happened in each apostle's last years.

What finally persuaded them to launch out in obedience to the bottom line of our Lord's last great command? Was it their reading of Luke's "how to" book—the Acts of the Apostles—that helped them to believe at last that they could indeed reach other peoples with the gospel, as Paul and Barnabas were doing?

Or was the destruction of Jerusalem by Titus in A.D. 70 the final persuasion that forced them out of their nest once and for all? Whatever the persuasion, most of them did finally move out! And ever since at least some Christians have kept moving out in obedience to Jesus' final command. Not all Christians, mind you. Only a small minority have obeyed the last great command in each generation. But that small minority of Christians has been for 2,000 years the single most powerful determiner of human history!

We hold in our hands the possibility of bringing God's 4,000-year-old promise to final fruition. Representing the Abraham factor, shunning all alliance with the Sodom factor and acknowledging the Melchizedek factor with the tithe of credit it deserves—

WE CAN DO IT!

Author's Postscript

Published in several languages since its first release in 1981, *Eternity in Their Hearts* is about to *burst from a cocoon*, so to speak, wearing a new, even more attractive, cover.

I am humbled and delighted by the response of readers worldwide to *Eternity in Their Hearts*. I cannot count the number of reports I have received of Christians who, after reading this book, have volunteered for missionary service or have resolved to support Christian missions. Other readers who shunned cross-cultural evangelism on the home front as too daunting have been emboldened to reach out to foreign refugees or immigrants in their neighborhoods. And other readers have been restored to faith after balking at impressions that God has left a majority of mankind without any witness whatsoever.

I am also heartened to learn of other researchers—some of them drawing cues from the 27 case studies in *Eternity in Their Hearts*—compiling and publishing their own evidences of "redemptive analogies" in diverse fields.

The primary thesis that I advocate in the book is a simple one: God's *general* revelation (see Ps. 19:1-4; Rom. 1:19-21; 2:14-15) is not an effete, inconsequential, inert bystander watching from the sidelines as God accomplishes everything related to redemption *via special revelation alone.* Instead, cosmic general revelation and canonized special revelation turn out to be stunningly coordinated players serving on the same team. God, via general revelation, *imprints* human cultures in a variety of ways. Discerning the particular way God has already imprinted a given culture helps a missionary discover how to poignantly explain redemption to members of that culture.

Just when I think that I know every possible way God foreshadows redemption in human cultures, He surprises me. I learned recently of belief in India about *an upside-down tree*—a tree that is upside-down because it is *rooted in heaven.* That tree's branches reach down to Earth, bearing fruit for mankind. The trunk of the upside-down tree, moreover, has been *gashed*. Sap bleeding from the wound in the side of the upside-down tree offers healing to mankind.

More and more similar discoveries keep turning up.

The sequel to *Eternity in Their Hearts* has been published at last, albeit with a rather different content that I originally planned. September 11, 2001, shifted my focus more to what I call the "Islamic Holocaust" than any of the other issues I originally intended to discuss. The result was *Secrets of the Koran*—my unavoidably disturbing analysis not only of the content of the Koran but also of tragic and oh-so-regrettable turning points in the life of Mohammed that still bode ill for millions living today.

There is one chapter in *Secrets of the Koran*, however, that overflows with much of what I originally intended to include in the sequel for *Eternity in Their Hearts*. It is the chapter called "Louis Farrakhan, Islam and Slavery"—chapter 15. A missionary from Africa assured me that, if necessary, he would gladly pay the price of *Secrets of the Koran* for just that fifteenth chapter.

My publisher asked if I would prefer—for safety's sake—to author *Secrets of the Koran* under a pseudonym. I replied that writing about Islam under pseudonyms—as many other authors do—is a capitulation to the arrogance of Muslim terrorists. Our capitulations must stop.

The time has come for us—in defense of the hard-won, easily-lost freedoms we still have—to respond. I am calling for a long-overdue media barrage to bring to light facts enshrined in Islamic history in which Mohammed discredits himself, the Koran, the Hadith and Islam's Shariah Law—in other words, the core of Islam itself!

The very nature of Islam as expressed in the Koran, the Hadith, Shariah Law and the example of Mohammed himself warn us that *we have no choice*.

Will such an exposé bring *spiritual* harm to Muslims impacted by it? In fact, it could not add one iota to the spiritual blight Islam itself brings upon Muslims. For many Muslims, discovering the true nature of their supposed prophet and the Koran will prove an antidote to their bondage.

Redemptive antidotes to human bondage are what *Eternity in Their Hearts* is all about. Indeed, in their hearts, truly seeking Muslims also long for release from the fear that Mohammed and the Koran instill but cannot assuage.

Don Richardson
2005

Endnotes

Chapter 1

1. A writer named Petronius, visiting Athens in the first century, was startled by the excessive number of gods in the city. Later he wrote that it was easier to find a god in Athens than it was to find a man! See Albert Barnes, *Notes on the Old & New Testaments* (Grand Rapids, MI: Baker Book House, 1982), relative to Acts 17:16.
2. Ibid.
3. Diogenes Laertius, *The Lives of Eminent Philosophers*, trans. R. D. Hicks for the Loeb Classical Library (London: Harvard University Press, 1925), vol. 1, p. 110.
4. See, for example, *Encyclopaedia Britannica*, 15th ed. (Chicago, IL: Encyclopaedia Britannica, 1974), vol. 13, p. 951 and vol. 14, p. 538.
5. Ibid., vol. 3, p. 924.
6. *The New Zondervan Pictorial Encyclopedia of the Bible*, vol. 4, Merrill C. Tenney, ed. (Grand Rapids, MI: Zondervan Publishing Company, 1974), pp. 177-178.
7. Ibid.
8. Ibid.
9. Victor W. Von Hagen, *The Ancient Sun Kingdoms of the Americas* (New York: World Publishing Co., 1957), p. 497.
10. Philip Ainsworth Means, "The Incas: Empire Builders of the Andes," *Indians of the Americas*, rev. ed. (Washington, D.C.: National Geographic Society, 1965), p. 307.
11. Alfred Metraux, *History of the Incas* (Westminster, MD: Pantheon Books, Random House, Inc., 1969), p. 123.
12. Hiram Bingham, "Discovering Machu Picchu," *Indians of the Americas*, p. 317.
13. Metraux, *History of the Incas*, p. 126.
14. Ibid., p. 128.
15. Ibid.
16. Means, "The Incas: Empire Builders of the Andes," *Indians of the Americas*, p. 306.
17. B. C. Brundage, *Empire of the Inca* (Norman, OK: University of Oklahoma Press, 1963), pp. 164-165.
18. Metraux, *History of the Incas*, p. 128.
19. Brundage, *Empire of the Inca*, p. 162.
20. Ibid., p. 163.
21. Ibid., p. 165.
22. Means, "The Incas: Empire Builders of the Andes," *Indians of the Americas*, pp. 305-306.
23. Brundage, *Empire of the Inca*, p. 165.
24. Metraux, *History of the Incas*, p. 126.
25. Leonard Cottrell, ed., *The Horizon Book of Lost Worlds* (New York: American Heritage Publishing Co., 1962), p. 115.
26. Lars Skrefsrud, *Traditions and Institutions of the Santal*, 1887.
27. Ibid.
28. Helen Gebuhr Ludvigsen, *All Heart* (Blair, NE: Lutheran Publishing House, 1952), n.p.

29. B. C. Brundage, *Lords of the Cuzco* (Norman, OK: University of Oklahoma Press, 1967), p. 143.

30. James Hastings, ed., *Encyclopedia of Religion and Ethics* (Edinburgh, UK: Clark 1908-1926), vol. 6, p. 272.

31. Comments on Confucianism, Taoism and Buddhism are taken from the *Encyclopaedia Britannica*.

32. John Ross, *History of Corea* (London: Elliot Stock, 62, Paternoster Row, 1891), p. 356.

33. From a personal interview with Mrs. John Tolliver at Three Hills, Alberta, April 1978. Mrs. Tolliver was raised in Korea and heard various references to this altar during her youth.

34. Spencer J. Palmer, *Korea and Christianity* (Seoul, South Korea: Hollym Corporation, 1967), p. 9.

35. "South Korea: Religion," *Wikipedia*, 2003 census data. http://en.wikipedia.org/wiki/South_Korea.

36. "Yoido Full Gospel Church—History: 1973-present," *Wikipedia*, 2003 census data. http://en.wikipedia.org/Yoido_Full_Gospel_Church.

37. Tricia Trillin, "The Transforming Church: David Yonggi Cho," *Cross+Word*, 1997 census data. http://www.intotruth.org/apostasy/cell-church4.htm#cho.

38. "The World's Largest Churches," *DAWN Fridayfax*, 2004, #36, compiled by Wolfgang Simson. http://www.jesus.org.uk/dawn/2004/dawn36.html.

39. "South Korea: Religion," *Wikipedia*, 2003 census data.

40. A further example of people who had a concept of the Vague God is related in *Bruchko* by Bruce Olson (Lake Mary, FL: Charisma House, 1977).

Chapter 2

1. Mrs. Macleod Wylie, *The Gospel in Burma* (London: W. H. Dalton, 1859), pp. 52-54.

2. Francis Mason, *The Karen Apostle* (Boston: Gould and Lincoln, 1861), p. 10.

3. Wylie, *The Gospel in Burma*, p. 22.

4. Mason, *The Karen Apostle*, p. 97.

5. Wylie, *The Gospel in Burma*, p. 6.

6. Alonzo Bunker, *Soo Thah, A Tale of the Karens* (New York: Fleming H. Revell Co., 1902), pp. 84-93.

7. Mason, *The Karen Apostle*, p. 99.

8. Ibid., p. 21.

9. Ibid., pp. 15-27.

10. Bunker, *Soo Thah, A Tale of the Karens*, p. 82.

11. Herman G. Tegenfeldt, *A Century of Growth, The Kachin Baptist Church of Burma* (Pasadena, CA: William Carey Library, 1974), p. 44.

12. Ibid., p. 45.

13. Ibid., p. 46.

14. From a personal interview with Nelda Widlund in 1980. Mrs. Widlund is the granddaughter of William Marcus Young.

15. Alexander MacLeish, *Christian Progress in Burma* (London: World Dominion Press, 1929), p. 52.

16. From a personal interview with Nelda Widlund and her father, Vincent Young.

17. From a personal interview with Alex C. Smith, doctor of missiology, Overseas Christian Fellowship.
18. MacLeish, *Christian Progress in Burma*, p. 51.
19. Ibid.
20. Ibid.
21. Ibid.
22. Phyllis Thompson, *James Frazer and the King of the Lisu* (Chicago: Moody Press, 1962), p. 64.
23. Tegenfeldt, *A Century of Growth*, p. 45.
24. Ibid., p. 46.
25. Hminga, *The Life and Witness of Churches in Mizoram* (Pasadena, CA: William Carey Library, 1976), pp. 31,42.
26. Tegenfeldt, *A Century of Growth*, p. 46.
27. Mason, *The Karen Apostle*, pp. 9-10.
28. Wylie, *The Gospel in Burma*, p. 86.
29. Mason, *The Karen Apostle*, p. 12.
30. Wylie, *The Gospel in Burma*, pp. 52-53.
31. Ibid., p. 52.
32. Ibid., p. 54.
33. Hugo Adolf Bernatzik, *The Spirits of Yellow Leaves*, E. W. Dickes, trans. (London: Robert Hale Ltd., 1951), n.p.
34. C. Peter Wagner, *On the Crest of the Wave* (Ventura, CA: Regal Books, 1983).
35. Hugo Adolf Bernatzik, *The Spirits of Yellow Leaves,* n.p.
36. "Nagaland," *Wikipedia,* 2001 census data. http://en.wikipedia.org/wiki/Nagaland.
37. "Our India: Christian Percentage in States," *Agape Bible Church, India,* 2001 census data. http://www.agapeindia.com/india_groups.htm.

Chapter 3

1. From interviews with Elmer Warkentin and his sons, and with Clara Lima, missionaries with RBMU International, working among the Dyak people of Kalimantan (Borneo).
2. Don Richardson, *Peace Child* (Ventura, CA: Regal Books, 2005), pp. 26-36.
3. Ibid., p. 241.
4. Don Richardson, *Lords of the Earth* (Ventura, CA: Regal Books, 1977), pp. 132-134.

Chapter 4

1. Edward B. Tylor, *Primitive Culture: Researches into the Development of Mythology, Philosophy, Religion, Art and Custom* (London: John Murray Publishers Ltd., 1871).
2. For a more detailed summary of Tylor's theory, see Fr. Wilhelm Schmidt, *The Origin and Growth of Religion* (New York: The Dial Press, 1931), pp. 74-77.
3. Ibid., pp. 74,77.
4. Ibid., pp. 78.
5. Ibid.
6. Ibid., pp. 170-171.
7. E. De Pressense, *A Study of Origins* (London: Hodder and Stoughton, 1887), pp. v-vi. First published in French in 1882.

8. Ibid., pp. vi-viii.
9. Ibid., p. viii.
10. Schmidt, *The Origin and Growth of Religion*, pp. 172-174.
11. Ibid., pp. 167-168.
12. Ibid., p. 174.
13. Ibid., p. 175.
14. Ibid., pp. 87-88.
15. Ibid., p. 88.
16. Ibid., p. 183.
17. Ibid., p. 70.
18. Ibid., pp. 192-193.
19. "Boas," *Encyclopaedia Britannica*, 15th ed. (Chicago, IL: Encyclopaedia Britannica, 1974).
20. See Hank Paulson and Don Richardson, *Beyond the Wall* (Ventura, CA: Regal Books, 1982).
21. *The Collected Works of Lenin*, trans. from German by H. Paulson, vol. 12 (n.p.: n.d.), p. 245.

Questions for Study

Chapter 1

1. Who was Epimenides? Which three assumptions were implicit in his unusual sacrifice?
2. Compare Gideon's "putting out the fleece" (Judg. 6:36-40) with Epimenides "putting out the whole flock." Is this general method for finding God's will still valid today? Have you ever used a similar approach? What were the results?
3. How did Paul react to the idolatry in Athens? On what basis did he adopt a very different attitude toward a certain altar in the city? In what sense does idolatry have a "built-in inflation factor"?
4. What is the Septuagint? What major problem did its translators have to face? What solution did they find? Did the apostles agree with their solution?
5. What evidence indicates that the apostle Paul was familiar with the story of Epimenides, and actually respected him?
6. Besides *theos*, what other familiar Greek term became an acceptable name for deity, and on what basis? Which apostle popularized the use of that term for Christians?
7. Who were Inti and Pachacuti and on what basis did the latter question the former's credentials?
8. What major political problem hindered Pachacuti's reformation? Could he have found a better solution to that problem?
9. In what way did European Christians betray the Aztecs, the Mayas and the Incas even more seriously than did Cortez, Pizarro and other conquistadores?
10. Compare the spiritual discernment of the Pharaoh Akhenaten with that of the Inca Pachacuti. Why do you think secular scholars have virtually ignored one while acclaiming the other?
11. Trace parallels between Old Testament and Santal accounts of human origins.

12. What biblical precedent mentioned earlier justifies Skrefsrud's acceptance of *Thakur Jiu* as a valid name for the Almighty among the Santal?

13. How have theologians in general reacted to news of the world-wide "sky-god" phenomenon? How did theologians unwittingly play into the hands of evolutionists?

14. How did the folk religion of the Gedeo people in Ethiopia prepare the way for the gospel?

15. What caused missionary Eugene Rosenau to exclaim that the Mbaka people were closer to the truth than his own forefathers in northern Europe?

16. What is meant by "redemptive lore"? Why not call it "redeeming lore"?

17. In what major way does the Great Commission run counter to human pride?

18. What major error in the thinking of early Chinese theologians opened the door and allowed Confucianism, Taoism and Buddhism to supplant the original worship of *Shang Ti/Hananim*?

19. How has Christianity tried to correct that ancient error?

20. Why did Protestant missionaries in Korea make faster initial progress than Catholic missionaries and what did the Catholics finally do to try to catch up?

Chapter 2

1. Trace parallels between the Bible and the amazing folk religions of the Karen, Kachin, Lahu, Wa, Lisu, Naga and Mizo peoples. What main emphases of the Bible were missing in those folk religions?

2. In what manner did these various folk religions anticipate God's provision of further revelation to fill in that which was lacking?

3. What major disadvantages did Ko Thah-byu overcome through God's grace, and what did he accomplish that caused him to be called "the Karen apostle"? What did the Karen peo-

ple as a whole contribute to peoples around them?

4. In what ways did Professor Hugo Bernatzik misread the true situation among the Kachin and Lahu peoples?

5. What scriptural basis do we have for accepting the existence of unusually enlightened pagans such as Epimenides, Pachacuti, Kolean, Pu Chan, Worassa and so on, as evidence of a sort of *illuminati* scattered by God to give witness that prepares the way for the gospel?

Chapter 3

1. What fascinating aspect of Gentile cultures caught Paul's eye, and how did he account for it?

2. How does Paul's observation help us to better understand Dyak culture in Borneo, the Asmat and the Yali cultures of Irian Jaya (New Guinea), and the culture of ancient Hawaii?

3. In what way did Asmat headhunter-cannibals of Irian Jaya have Nicodemus the Jew over a barrel?

4. Give two examples of biblical concepts apparently encoded within Chinese pictographs.

5. Explain the *sacred four* concept. How do North American Indian tribes symbolize the sacred four?

6. In what ways does the Bible honor the number four? What theological parallels offer better access for the gospel to the Indian mind?

Chapter 4

1. How did Edward Tylor apply Darwin's theory of evolution to explain the rise of religion? What evidence gathered from around the world refutes Tylor's theory? How did early evolutionists respond to that evidence? Name two ethnologists of the early twentieth century who sought to publicize the contradicting evidence.

2. Name two major implications of Tylor's theory and show how each implication, carried to its logical conclusions by certain individuals, resulted in disaster.

3. What warning should ideological innovators take from the above case study?

4. What recent historical developments are tending to correct the disastrous effects of Tylor's theory?

Chapter 5

1. Explain the mutual complementarity of the top and bottom lines of the Abrahamic Covenant.

2. Toward what had God "targeted" the blessing mentioned in "the bottom line"? Name some Old Testament narratives which show sons and daughters of Abraham working out the bottom line of the covenant.

3. What passages indicate that the apostles Paul and Peter and the writer of the Epistle to the Hebrews saw the Abrahamic Covenant (including its bottom line) as foundational to the New Testament era?

Chapter 6

1. Name some ways in which Jesus revealed His total commitment to the bottom line of the Abrahamic Covenant throughout His ministry, not just at the last minute before His ascension.

2. On the basis of Matthew 10:5-6 and 15:24, some say that Jesus came to offer the Jews a literal, physical kingdom, giving them exclusive dominion over the Gentiles then and there, and that He resorted to the Great Commission only as a sort of "plan B"—after the Jews rejected the plan He preferred. Discuss this theory in the light of Matthew 10:18 and other such Scriptures.

3. Describe instances when Jesus used encounters with non-Jewish people to teach an all-peoples perspective.

Chapter 7

1. In what way was deacon Philip's ministry so crucial?

2. Cite passages in Acts that show that the 12 apostles were still

subliminally if not overtly reluctant to obey the bottom line of the Great Commission.

3. What was very probably Luke's barely hidden motive for writing Acts?

4. What were Paul's two new ideas? How does a church differ from a synagogue? How does a missionary band differ from a church?

5. What was shockingly unfair about the agreement described in Galatians 2:9?

6. What "final persuasions" may God have used to stir the apostles out of their nest at Jerusalem?

Bibliography

Bavinck, J. H. *An Introduction to the Science of Missions*. Translated by David H. Freeman. Nutley, NJ: Presbyterian and Reformed Publishing Co., 1977. Bavinck, tending to discredit the importance of biblical parallels in pagan cultures represents what might be called the "old school approach" to missionary communication.

Bennett, Wendall and Junius Bird. *Andean Culture History*. Lancaster, PA: Lancaster Press, Inc., 1949 and 1960.

Bernatzik, Hugo Adolf, with the collaboration of Emmy Bernatzik. *The Spirits of the Yellow Leaves*. Translated by E. W. Dickes. London: Robert Hale Limited, 1951.

Bruce, F. F. *The Spreading Flame: The Rise and Progress of Christianity*. Grand Rapids: Wm. B. Eerdmans Publishing Co., 1958.

Brundage, B. C. *Empire of the Inca*. Norman, OK: University of Oklahoma Press, 1963.

_____. *Lords of the Cuzco*. Norman, OK: University of Oklahoma Press, 1967.

Bunker, Alonzo. *Soo Thah—A Tale of the Karens*. New York: Fleming H. Revell Co., 1902.

Cottrell, Leonard. *The Horizon Book of the Lost Worlds*. New York: American Heritage Publishing Co., 1962.

Frazer, Gordon. *Symposium on Creation V*. Edited by Donald W. Patten. Grand Rapids: Baker Book House, 1975.

Fuller, Harold W. *Run While the Sun Is Hot*. Cedar Grove: Sudan Interior Mission, 1967.

Howard, Randolph L. *Baptists in Burma*. Philadelphia: The Judson Press, 1931.

_____. *It Began in Burma*. Philadelphia: The Judson Press, 1942.

Jacobson, Daniel. *Great Indian Tribes*. Maplewood, NJ: Hammond, Inc., 1970.

Kang, C. H., and Ethyl R. Nelson. *The Discovery of Genesis*. St. Louis: Concordia Publishing House, 1979.

Laertius, Diogenes. *Lives of Eminent Philosophers*. 2 vols. Translated by R. D. Hicks for the Loeb Classical Library. London: Harvard University Press, 1925.

Latourette, Kenneth Scott. *A History of Christianity, Beginnings to 1500, Volume 1*. New York: Harper and Row Publishers, 1953.

_____. *A History of Christianity, Reformation to the Present, Volume 2*. Harper and Row Publishers, 1953.

Lutz, Larry. *The Mizos—God's Hidden People*. San Jose, CA: Christian Nationals Evangelism Commission, Inc., 1980.

McBirnie, William Stuart. *The Search for the Twelve Apostles*. Wheaton, IL: Tyndale House Publishers, Inc., 1973.

MacLeish, Alexander. *Christian Progress in Burma*. London: World Dominion Press, 1929.

Mason, Francis. *The Karen Apostle*. Boston: Gould and Lincoln, 1861.

Mayers, Marvin K. *Christianity Confronts Culture*. Grand Rapids: Zondervan Publishing House, 1974.

Murphree, Marshall W. *Christianity and the Shona*. London: The Athlone Press, University of London, 1969.

Olson, Bruce E. *Bruchko*. Carol Stream, IL: Creation House, 1973.

Palmer, Spencer J. *Korea and Christianity*. Korea: Hollym Corporation, 1967.

Purser, William Charles Bertrand. *Christian Missions in Burma*. Westminster, England: Society of the Propagation of the Gospel in Foreign Parts, 1913.

Ray, Verne F. *Primitive Pragmatists: The Modoc Indians of Northern California*. Seattle and London: University of Washington Press, 1963.

Richardson, Don. *Lords of the Earth*. Ventura, CA: Regal Books, 1977.

_____. *Peace Child*. Ventura, CA: Regal Books, 1974.

Schmidt, Wilhelm. *Primitive Revelation*. Translated by Joseph Abierl. St. Louis: R. Herder, 1939.

Stickley, Caroline. *Broken Snare*. London: Overseas Missionary Fellowship, 1975.

Tegenfeldt, Herman G. *A Century of Growth—The Kachin Baptist Church of Burma*. South Pasadena, CA: William Carey Library, 1974.

Thompson, Phyllis. *James Fraser and the King of the Lisu*. Chicago: Moody Press, 1962.

Tylor, Edward Burnett. *Researches into the Early History of Mankind and the Development of Civilization*, 1865.

_____. *Primitive Culture*, 1871.

Smith, Alex G. *Strategy to Multiply Rural Churches—A Central Thailand Case Study*. Bangkok: O. M. F. Publishers, 1977.

Von Hagen, Victor W. *The Ancient Sun Kingdoms of the Americas*. Cleveland and New York: World Publishing Co., 1957.

Weiss, G. Christian. *The Heart of Missionary Theology*. Chicago: Moody Press, 1976, 1977.

Wylie, Mrs. Macleod. *The Gospel in Burma*. London: W. H. Dalton, Bookseller to the Queen, 1859.

More of the Best
from Don Richardson

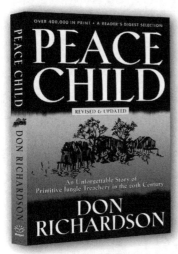
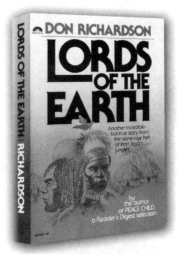
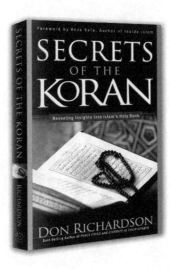